ORCHID
FEVER

ORCHID
FEVER

A HORTICULTURAL TALE

OF LOVE, LUST,

AND LUNACY

Eric Hansen

Pantheon Books New York

5/00

Pantheon Books and colophon are registered trademarks
of Random House, Inc.

A portion of this work appeared in different form
in *Natural History* magazine.

Library of Congress Cataloging-in-Publication Data

Hansen, Eric.
Orchid fever : a horticultural tale of love, lust, and lunacy /
Eric Hansen.
p.   cm.
ISBN 0-679-45141-2
1. Plant collectors—Anecdotes.   2. Nursery growers—
Anecdotes.   3. Orchid industry—Anecdotes.
4. Orchids—Anecdotes.   5. Hansen, Eric.   I. Title.
SB61 .H36   2000
635.9'344—dc21   99-044582

Random House Web Address: www.randomhouse.com

Book design by Fearn Cutler de Vicq
Illustrations by Tim Purus

Printed in the United States of America
FIRST EDITION
2 4 6 8 9 7 5 3 1

For

DelRae and Gunnar

You can get off alcohol, drugs, women, food, and cars, but once you're hooked on orchids, you're finished. You never get off orchids . . . never.

Joe Kunisch
Commercial orchid grower
Rochester, New York

CONTENTS

Contents

ORCHID
FEVER

Chapter 1

JOURNEY TO
FIRE MOUNTAIN

Paphiopedilum sanderianum

There is something distinctive about the sight and sound of a human body falling from the rain forest canopy. The breathless scream, the wildly gyrating arms and legs pumping thin air, the rush of leaves, snapping branches, and the sickening thud, followed by uneasy silence. Listening to that silence, I reflected on how plant collecting can be an unpleasant sort of activity.

Bits of debris continued to fall from the trees and I could make out a faint plume of dust, caught in a shaft of sunlight, that indicated where the body had landed. A nearby sapling swayed back and forth a few times, then stood still. In the distance, obscured by the steaming labyrinth of trees and climbing woody vines, a cicada began its shrieking high-pitched call. The rain forest suddenly felt much closer and far less friendly than it had just a few moments earlier. Sweat dripped from my chin, and I held my breath to halt my growing sense of panic. Then I heard the first moan of pain, and all sense of time and fear was swept away.

Earlier that day, I had entered the Borneo rain forest in search of wild orchids. The morning mist was still rising and the dawn bird chorus had just faded as Tiong, a government plant collector, and two of his helpers paused at the base of a limestone cliff to burn joss sticks and stacks of Chinese devotional money. These offerings were intended to appease the spirit world before we started our climb. Everything began well enough, but by midday the mountain spirits responded to our presence. Tiong was near the top of a tree when he reached up and gripped a Wragler's pit viper sleeping on a branch. Within moments, my guide and protector was hurtling through space with two fang marks in the back of his hand. We didn't find the orchids we were looking for, and we spent the rest of the afternoon trying to get Tiong off the mountain. Tiong lived, but after that experience, I felt confident that I wouldn't be participating in any more orchid-hunting trips.

My journey with Tiong was part of a plan that I had come up with to build an upriver plant nursery for a group of indigenous people known as the Penan. Members of this tribe had helped me to walk across the island of Borneo in 1982 during a six-month-long, 1,500-mile cross-country journey. At the time, many of the Penan were still nomadic hunters and gatherers and I traveled with them in order to experience a vanishing way of life. The journey nearly cost me my life, but in the end I returned home and wrote my first book, *Stranger in the Forest*. During that harrowing journey, the Penan taught me how to survive, but more important, they showed me a different way of being, and my life has never been quite the same since then. For years I have felt a profound debt of gratitude to these people. Today, most Penan lead settled lives in remote villages. They are not farmers, and without language or business skills they have no steady source of income apart from working as migrant laborers for logging or mining companies. They are highly skilled at collecting jungle products from the primary rain forest, and this got me to thinking. Years went by, but I eventually came up with the idea that a small commercial nursery filled with exotic jungle plants salvaged from the nearby logging concessions might be the perfect financial solution for them.

The only problem was that I knew absolutely nothing about how to start or maintain a nursery, and I didn't know which plants might be of horticultural interest, or which species were valuable. I also had no idea that international regulations prohibited such a venture. I continued to think about the village nursery idea, and this is why I eventually ended up on top of the mountain with Tiong. I wanted him to educate me in the fine art of collecting wild orchids and other desirable plants. As it turned out, Tiong went to the hospital, where he was put on a respirator, and I returned home to rethink my village nursery scheme.

Six months later I received a letter from Richard Baskin, an orchid grower in Minneapolis. I had no idea who the man was, but a friend had told him I knew all about upriver travel in Borneo. Richard wanted to know if I would take him and a friend, Donald Levitt, an orchid grower from North Dakota, to the Borneo rain forest to look for an orchid known as *Paphiopedilum* (pronounced "paf-ee-oh-pedilum") *sanderianum*. It seemed a long way to go for the sake of looking at a plant that might not be in flower, but I phoned him a few days later to discuss the idea. In the back of my mind, I thought these two men might teach me something about orchids and help me with the village nursery idea.

"It's the holy grail of orchids," Richard explained. "Maybe only a dozen botanists on earth have seen it bloom in the wild. It has the whole orchid world in turmoil. Conservationists, scientists, and commercial growers are at each other's throats over the plant."

Orchid world in turmoil? I had no idea what the orchid world was, let alone how such a thing could be in turmoil or why I should get involved with another orchid hunt. At the time, I couldn't distinguish a *Phalaenopsis* from an *Odontoglossum*, but from dozens of visits to Borneo over the previous eighteen years I knew the isolated mountain area that Richard and Donald wanted to visit. I had the time, they had the money, and three months later we stood ankle-deep in mud at the edge of a jungle river in Sarawak, the East Malaysian state on the island of Borneo. We were one hundred miles upriver, one hundred years back in time, and judging from the childlike looks of wonderment on my companions' faces, we had arrived in orchid heaven. Then the little men with the spears arrived.

I introduced the two orchidophiles to my diminutive Penan friends—Bati and Katong. Like all Penan they are masters of the deep forest, and I had traveled hundreds of miles through the jungle with Bati and Katong over the previous ten years. I had sent word of our plans to them by way of an upriver trading post. The message was for them to meet us at the junction of the Limbang and Medalam rivers on the full moon of the fourth month of 1993.

Bati and Katong have never seen a compass or a map, but what they don't know about hunting dogs, the use of a spear, or long-distance jungle travel isn't worth knowing. They can build a waterproof shelter from leaves in twenty minutes, catch fish with their feet, and light a fire without matches in a tropical downpour. The forest is their home. It is the setting for their creation myths, the resting place of their ancestors, and, until recently, an unlimited storehouse of food, medicine, and building material. To the average Western visitor, the Borneo rain forest is a chaotic, steaming green hell of leeches, biting insects, giant cockroaches, bad smells, and certain death. Bati and Katong speak no English, so it was my job to translate and to try to explain the purpose of our trip to these two jungle men.

"They have come twelve thousand miles to look at a flower?" Bati asked me in Malay.

"It is true," I replied.

"Can you eat this flower?" Katong asked.

"No."

"Is it used for medicine?"

"No."

"What do they want to do with this flower?"

"Take photographs and measure the leaves."

"And how much have these men paid to come look at the flower?"

"About $3,500 each," I said.

Having established these basic facts, Bati and Katong retreated into a special Penan silence that suggests indifference or nonchalance, but in fact is an expression of profound disbelief.

Once we had the dugout canoe loaded, a quick look at the orchid hunters' baggage pretty well said all there was to say about our respective cultures. Donald had brought a sling psychrometer for measuring relative humidity, an altimeter, litmus paper, a handheld Satellite Global Positioning System for establishing the precise latitude and longitude of any orchid on earth—within ten feet. Or was it ten inches? I can't remember. Then there were the video camera and still cameras and all their accessories, a compass, tape recorders, batteries and battery rechargers, binoculars, electrolyte balancers, Powerbars, sunblock, water purification tablets, a hand pump for filtering water, dental floss, hair shampoo and conditioners, deodorants, breath fresheners, hiking boots, recently purchased adventure-travel clothing, and insect repellent. They had freeze-dried food, inflatable sleeping mattresses and pillows, mosquito nets, rolls of toilet paper, rip-stop nylon tents, Cordura cloth cot stretchers, a stove-top espresso maker, canteens, tripods, notebooks, umbrellas, plastic tea cups, and digital wristwatches. Donald put on a pair of wraparound sunglasses with mirrored lenses and then won the prize for weirdness with a shrink-wrapped collapsible toilet made from die-cut sections of camouflaged cardboard.

The Penan had brought a cooking pot, two spear-tipped blowguns, a quiver of poisoned darts, and jungle knives. They also carried two empty backpacks, which was just as well, because they would need all the space they could find in those backpacks to haul the orchid hunters' equipment through the jungle.

We shoved off from shore and continued our journey into the remote interior of the island. The Medalam River was in flood. We slowly motored against the brown current, which was littered with tangles of uprooted vegetation and floating logs. Scattered along this winding green corridor of giant trees, the branches were laden with pitcher plants and flowering orchids.

"*Dimorphorchis lowii,*" Donald called out, as he slapped at a mosquito on his forehead.

Then Richard spotted *Dayakia hendersoniana,* and *Grammatophyllum speciosum,* the largest orchid on earth. They continued their roll call of Borneo orchids and eventually fell into a heated discussion that startled our Penan guides.

"*Arachnanthe!*" Donald blurted out, his face flushed with excitement.

"Try *Dimorphorchis,* you dinosaur," Richard shouted back. This comment unleashed an exchange of taxonomic firepower that ended in an uncomfortable silence. It was the sort of botanical nit-picking that I would listen to for the duration of the trip.

"Are they going to fight?" Katong asked.

"No, they are just discussing the name of a flower," I told him.

Farther upriver, Donald lowered his binoculars to give his eyes a rest, and told us a story about how a disgruntled customer (an entomologist who made a living synthesizing the scent of the female fruit fly in heat) had accused him of selling diseased plants. To further emphasize his point the man had beaten Donald unconscious in his greenhouse. Then Richard explained how two California orchid growers had settled an argument about intergeneric hybridizing with a two-foot length of water pipe and a burst of gunfire. One man had died. When I translated these stories for Bati and Katong, they remarked that orchid growing sounded like a dangerous business.

Late that afternoon, we pulled the longboat onto a sandy bank and hauled our bags ashore. Bati set up a temporary shelter from leaves and cut saplings while Katong went off into the jungle in search of food. He returned a short time later with a neatly wrapped bundle of fiddlehead ferns tied up in a leaf and a load of wild jackfruit called *buah nakan*. He also produced a three-foot-long tree root known as *Tonkat Ali* (*Eurycoma longifolia*)—the fabled Walking Stick of Ali. According to Katong, a tea made from the sliced root enables a man to make love five times in a single night. "More useful than orchid," Katong explained.

We divided up the root for later use, and after a dinner of fresh fish, sautéed fiddlehead ferns, steamed rice, and jackfruit, we opened our first bottle of *tuak* (rice wine). Sitting back to enjoy the spectacle of hundreds of fireflies moving through the jungle night, we agreed that the journey had gotten off to an auspicious start.

That night at the campfire, Richard described *Paphiopedilum sanderianum*, the tropical lady's slipper orchid that we were looking for, and how the common name for the flower comes from the distinctive pouch that looks like a small slipper. The genus *Paphiopedilum* includes more than eighty species, ranging from India across China to the Philippines and throughout Southeast Asia and Indonesia to New Guinea and the Solomon Islands. Many of the best orchid habitat sites are in Sarawak and the one we were headed for was a place the Penan call Gunong Api (Fire Mountain). In 1993, Fire Mountain was accessible only by dugout canoe and on foot, a round-trip journey of ten days.

Paphiopedilum sanderianum is one of the most spectacular and sought-after orchids in the world. It is an unusual plant in that its flowers have two wavy, drooping petals that can reach more than three feet in length. In addition to its extraordinary floral display, the sanderianum has a colorful history. First discovered in the Sarawak rain forest by the German plant collector J. Förstermann in 1885, it was thought to have become extinct in the wild.

Richard pointed out that the orchid experts of the world had thought the plant was extinct in the wild because they didn't know where it grew and, because of the huge expense involved in mounting a botanical expedition, no one had spent any time searching for it. The orchid was "rediscovered" by accident in 1978 when the botanist Ivan Nielsen found it flowering near Fire Mountain. Ever since then the sanderianum has been championed by certain botanists and botanic institutions as one of the rarest of the rare; one of the most endangered plant species on earth.

As we traveled upriver in search of the sanderianum I was oblivious to the international fuss that surrounded the orchid; but Richard and Donald gradually filled me in on the petty and vicious world of plant politics. Largely as a result of publicity generated by the rediscovery of the sanderianum, a few orchid collectors started looking for where the plant grew. Until our trip in 1993 this was a secret carefully guarded by local villagers, several plant collectors, and a few botanists at the Royal Botanic Gardens, Kew. Naturally, at the time of its rediscovery in 1978, other scientific institutions, botanists, plant historians, and commercial growers wanted to get their hands on the sanderianum for research and artificial propagation. This sort of international excitement eventually aroused the attention of policymakers at CITES (pronounced "sigh-tees," the Convention on International Trade in Endangered Species of Wild Fauna and Flora), which has its headquarters in Geneva.

In December 1987, Henry Azadehdel, an orchid collector, was arrested at Heathrow Airport and charged with smuggling orchids. British and U.S. newspapers and magazines gave lurid descriptions of how orchid piracy and illegal trade were leading to the extinction of wild orchid species. The concept of orchid smuggling was entirely new to me, and I followed their version of events with a great deal of interest and skepticism.

Within less than a year the sanderianum was being promoted at CITES meetings as if it was as urgently in need of protection as the giant panda or the African elephant. One of the main problems with this analogy, according to Richard, was the simple fact that the trade laws don't distinguish between plants and animals. Endangered megafauna (elephants, rhinoceros, whales) might produce only one offspring per year, whereas a single sanderianum seed pod can produce about 8,000 to 10,000 seedlings per year in a commercial nursery, and a mature plant carries five to twenty pods. If whales, elephants, and rhinoceros had this sort of reproductive capability, there wouldn't be room on earth to put them or their steaming byproducts.

In 1989, the sanderianum and all remaining *Paphiopedilum* species were placed on what is known as CITES Appendix I, an official list of the most endangered species. There is a total ban on the international commercial trade of Appendix I wild plants and plant parts. This includes the pollen, flowers, seed pods, and leaves of those plants. The rule about parts, as it applies to plants, seemed odd because it was primarily designed to protect animals by stopping the trade in animal parts such as walrus tusks, python skins, elephant ivory, whale teeth, dried tiger penises, rhinoceros horns, and tortoise shell. From the viewpoint of plant conservation, I was curious to know what possible connection there could be between dried tiger penises and orchid seed pods.

"That remains a carefully guarded secret that orchid growers and botanists have been pondering for years," Richard said.

Stifling, languid days passed as we moved slowly upriver. At night we sat cross-legged at the campfire and continued to talk about the strange world of orchid conservation. One of the things that I found odd about the endangered orchid story was the fact that the sanderianum had been put on Appendix I without any hard data to support the claim that the plant populations were critically low, and that the species was endangered. I suggested to Richard that this didn't sound like a very scientific or logical way to go about protecting a species, but my comment merely revealed how little I knew about the politics of plant conservation.

"People are paid money to make laws to protect flowers?" Bati asked, looking up from his task of making poisoned darts. His knife handle was made from the femur of a long-tailed macaque.

In the case of *Paphiopedilum sanderianum,* no one had conducted a systematic population survey of the plant to establish whether, in fact, it was threatened with extinction, and if so, what was the nature of that threat. This complete absence of basic knowledge about how the plant grows in the wild and what conditions it needs to thrive was the reason that Donald and Richard wanted to find the sanderianum habitat. I also learned that essential scientific research is complicated or impeded by the CITES treaty or national laws that do not adequately distinguish between live and dead plants. For example, it is illegal, without import and export permits, to transport even pickled or dried Appendix I orchid herbarium specimens across most international borders. Richard described how a highly regarded German orchid taxonomist had recently been denied permission to import hundred-year-old dried orchid specimens for research purposes because they were listed on the CITES Appendix I list. The man tried to reason with the customs officer, explaining that the rules should apply only to live plants, but in the end he lost his patience and punched the customs officer in the face.

"Illegal to move dead plants from one place to another?" Katong asked. "Why?" Our Penan guides were dumbfounded by such regulations and I can't say that I blamed them. I was perplexed myself, and the more I heard, the more intrigued I became with the inner workings of the orchid world. Donald even mentioned that armed customs officers with attack dogs were raiding orchid nurseries in Europe, but I dismissed this tale as nothing more than the mindless ranting of an obsessed orchid fanatic.

The days passed; as we traveled farther into the forest in search of our legendary plant, the journey began to feel more and more like a quest for the ultimate botanical treasure on earth. The two orchid growers seemed willing to undergo any amount of exertion, excruciating pain, or discomfort on the off chance that we would find the plant in flower. Bati and Katong, on the other hand, were largely indifferent to the orchid hunt, which they saw as a silly way to spend one's time. They moved through the jungle collecting food and finding the way with an ease of spirit that was unnerving, especially to Donald, who spent much of his time looking for dry, bug-free, level places to set up his camouflaged cardboard toilet. When we weren't paddling up quiet backwaters or portaging the dugout over muddy slopes strung with rattan vines that ripped clothing and flesh like barbed wire, we sat around camp drinking tea, applying Band-Aids, talking about orchids, and trying to explain everyday life in the United States to our Penan guides. One afternoon, Richard produced a photo of his wife's six Afghan show dogs.

"So big," Bati exclaimed. "Are they good hunters?"

"Well, actually, they don't hunt," Richard said. "If they went outside they would get dirty and we would have to give them a bath. We keep them in the house. They have their own beds and we feed them dog food."

"What is dog food?" asked Bati.

Then Donald showed the Penan a photo of his orchid greenhouse covered with snow.

"What is snow?" Katong asked.

I explained snow as frozen rain that piles up on the ground for several months each year. I think they understood this, but the concept of buying food for dogs that don't hunt, or why someone would choose to live in a place where it snowed, was beyond them.

I told the two Penan about my idea for a village nursery. Bati considered this possibility and then asked how much a fully mature sanderianum plant would sell for in the United States. When Richard told him the figure ($2,000–$3,000), Bati announced that the sum represented more money than he would earn in his entire life. With this in mind, he asked why the Penan couldn't collect a few orchids each year to sell to foreign buyers. With the loggers, dam builders, farmers, hotel developers, and road builders closing in on the area, it seemed like a good idea. Unfortunately for the Penan and the orchids, as Richard pointed out, it is perfectly legal to flood an orchid habitat with a hydroelectric dam, log it, level the hillsides for a road, build a golf course on the site, or burn the jungle to the ground for agricultural purposes, but CITES influence and rules make it extremely difficult, if not impossible, to salvage the plants and sell them. I found this very hard to believe.

"If the rules say that no one can collect these plants, what will happen to them when the road builders, farmers, and loggers come?" Katong asked.

"The plants will die and the rules will live on," Richard said.

We arrived at the foot of Fire Mountain on the morning of our fifth day in the rain forest. Over the previous ten years, both Richard and Donald had dreamed of discovering a sanderianum plant flowering in the wild, and so there was a palpable sense of excitement in the air as we started up the steep slope. Bati and Katong cut a way through a wall of vegetation with their jungle knives, but the going was not easy as we climbed into a mist-filled mountain forest strewn with a jumble of knife-edged limestone formations.

After about an hour of pulling ourselves uphill by grasping slippery roots and limestone as sharp as glass, we reached a level piece of ground. Donald checked his altimeter and swung his sling psychrometer to get a humidity reading. Richard looked at his compass and then indicated the direction we should walk. Within fifteen minutes we arrived at a place where everything was right: the humidity, the light, the air flow, and the type of limestone cliffs where the sanderianum grows. We moved north along the foot of a west-facing cliff, and then strained our eyes as we looked up into the mass of vegetation above us. Off to one side, a cool breeze moved across the cliff face and sent a pair of unmistakable undulating petals into motion.

There was a moment of electrified silence before Donald sputtered out a phrase that sounded something like: "OH MY GOD I DON'T FUCKING BELIEVE IT WHERE'S MY CAMERA!"

"Mondo . . . ," said Richard.

We climbed to about 950 feet, where we were surrounded by hundreds of sanderianum plants. It was difficult to move around for fear of trampling on the orchids, so we stood still for a moment savoring the incredible sight of these pristine wild plants. Only a handful of people on earth had ever seen what lay before us.

"AGGGGGH WHERE THE HELL IS MY GOD-DAMN HIGH-SPEED FILM?" Donald screamed into his camera bag before dumping its contents onto the ground.

Once the two men had calmed down, they swung into action while Bati, Katong, and I sat back to drink in the scene of orchid ecstasy. Motor drives whirred, leaves were measured (3 inches across), mature plants, seedlings, and seed pods were counted, rainwater was tested (pH 6.3), light was measured in units of foot-candles (2,500 to 4,000 in patterned shade), and samples of rock (pH 7.5) and peat (pH 7.3) were tested. Four hours later we were on our way down the mountain with notebooks full of data. Over the course of a week, we returned to the site several times, and then moved on to discover thousands of sanderianum plants in dozens of different sites. I was surprised when Richard told me that this sort of independent research, without special permits from the host country, is also prohibited.

When Bati and Katong asked Richard what would happen if someone tried to take sanderianum plants back to the United States to sell on their behalf, he told them that the fine could be as high as $500,000 plus ten years in jail. Then they wanted to know how much people got paid to help make up such laws and punishments. Richard said that he knew of a plant conservationist who made more than $100,000 per year to help lay the groundwork for those penalties.

"Ah," they concluded, "no wonder the fines are so high. How else could the man's salary be paid?"

That wasn't quite right, but close enough.

The embers of the fire glowed a deep red as Bati and Katong let a respectful silence fall over the campsite. Things had become clearer for them, and perhaps they felt it was unnecessary to probe deeper into a culture where people shot each other for flowers, raised dogs that didn't hunt, and were cursed by a frozen rain that fell from the sky like pebbles.

Out in the jungle night, I saw the familiar sweeping beam of a flashlight. Donald was on the prowl once again, responding to another call of nature. The beam of light eventually came to rest. It illuminated the overhead canopy for a few minutes and then, without warning, everything went dark. I heard a distant rustle of leaves, a stifled cry, and what sounded like a body falling off a collapsible cardboard toilet. Bati and Katong looked at each other and then shook their heads. It was time to go home.

Chapter 2

BODICE RIPPERS

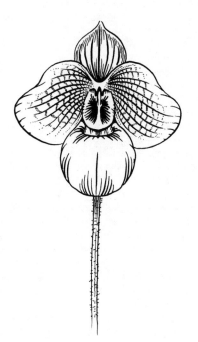

Paphiopedilum Magic Lantern

A cold wind rattled the windows as I sat at my writing table in San Francisco, bundled up against the winter morning chill. A foghorn on the Golden Gate Bridge droned in the distance as the swirling, damp mist cascaded over the rooftops and partly hid a row of Victorian façades across the street. Up under the eaves of my building I could see a line of roosting pigeons ruffling their feathers for warmth. I listened to their gentle cooing sounds, but my thoughts were far away on the steaming, fetid slopes of Fire Mountain.

By this time I had abandoned my idea of an orchid nursery for the Penan. The control of these plants seemed to be locked up by regulations that were conceived and enforced by people who lived half a world away. But I could not get Richard and Donald and their flower stories out of my mind. The images of rare orchid smugglers, vindictive botanists who double-crossed their colleagues, Ph.D. candidates fist-fighting with customs agents over dried plant specimens, and bizarre trade regulations enforced by a shadowy network of government officials who raided greenhouses with attack dogs and automatic weapons seemed too far-fetched to be true. But the stories were so wonderfully odd and the characters so perfectly eccentric and improbable that I found myself secretly hoping that there was some truth to what I had heard.

Writing up my field notes from the trip to Fire Mountain was hugely entertaining. I found myself laughing out loud as I thumbed through the crumpled and muddy pages of my spiral notebooks and relived our journey. I shared many of these stories with friends, but when it came to the task of double-checking facts and verifying events, I hesitated. I enjoyed the stories the way they had been told to me and felt no need to examine them more closely. This approach worked for a while, but before long my curiosity got to work and I could no longer resist the temptation to take a closer look at the world of the orchid people.

I started my search by visiting the library at the Strybing Arboretum and Botanical Garden in Golden Gate Park. Seated at a long hardwood desk, I thumbed through more than fifty years' worth of articles published in journals such as the *Orchid Digest* and *Orchids,* the magazine of the American Orchid Society. I immersed myself in the rarefied field of orchid research, and over the following days I started to discover some mighty strange things about the family Orchidaceae.

I read one paper titled "Pseudocopulation in Australian Terrestrial Orchids," by William Stoutamire, and another called "The Mechanism for the Maintenance of Species Integrity in Sympatrically Occurring Equitant Oncidiums in the Caribbean," by Lawrence Nierenberg. Another one of my favorites was "Ultraviolet Mimicry by Bulbophyllum Lepidum?," authored by Donald L. Koehler and Demorest Davenport. The arcane scientific terminology and the stiff, affected style of writing made for very heavy reading, but I was captivated by the passion of the authors. Their keen intelligence, narrow focus, and maniacal pursuit of orchid esoterica were breathtaking, and I eagerly followed them as they doggedly probed these murky botanical backwaters.

I had always thought of orchids in terms of corsages to be worn at high school proms in the 1950s, but as I read on I was confronted with scientific and scholarly papers describing orchids in an entirely new light. I was surprised to learn that they were also used in the making of foods, clothing, paint pigments, medicines, pig feed, religious charms, lubricants, adhesives, musical instruments, packaging, cosmetics, perfumes, and food flavorings (the vanilla bean). One paper, "The Orchid in Literature," by Martha Hoffman Lewis, described how Marcel Proust equated the plants with harlots and homosexuals, George Bernard Shaw compared them to courtesans, and John Ruskin, repelled by the blatant sexuality of the flowers, considered orchids to be "prurient apparitions." Another study was devoted entirely to listing orchid species mentioned in science fiction and mystery writing.

I learned that the Aztec emperor Montezuma cultivated the orchid *Stanhopea tigrina,* and that *Orchis maculata* was used as an aphrodisiac in late-medieval Iceland. On a similar note, the chewed stem of the *Lissochilus* orchid was known to produce powerful erections of the penis among Lobedu tribesmen in Transvaal as recently as 1962. In Malaysia the roots of *Cymbidium finlaysonianum* could cure a sick elephant, and a paste from the pulverized bulbs of certain species of *Cyrtopodium* was used as an adhesive by shoemakers in rural Guyana. I also discovered that the split pseudobulbs of *Coelogyne asperata* are made into blackboard erasers by rural schoolteachers in the villages of central Sumatra, and that children in Honduras fashion trumpets from the hollow stalks of *Schomburgkia tibicinis.*

In the remote mountains of Papua New Guinea, the Chimbu people call a certain *Dendrobium* species *duruagle.* The same name was given to a flirtatious female ghost who walked around naked and seduced young men. If you encountered the ghost and proved to be sexually incompetent, you had better find the orchid *duruagle* quickly, because it was the only known cure for a painful condition of the groin that afflicted those who couldn't satisfy the pretty ghost.

The sheer volume and range of written material on orchids was overwhelming. I even learned about orchids and the popular dating practices of Zulu tribesmen in 1932. According to several European observers, young Zulu men would place a leaf of the orchid *Ansellia africana* in their armpit during courtship. It was also important to have a supply of prepared roots of this plant on hand, because the concoction acted as an aphrodisiac and was thought to render unmarried women infertile for a night.

Stimulated by this overview of the history of orchids and the people who have studied and cultivated them, I moved on to the main branch of the San Francisco Public Library, where I tracked down what little had been written recently in the popular press about orchid pirates and international plant smugglers. In contrast to the meticulously researched papers that I had been reading about orchid history and biology, the newspaper coverage seemed shallow and a bit light on facts. But what was lacking in solid journalistic method was more than compensated for by the high level of righteous indignation. Most of the articles read like slightly reworded press releases sent out by a strident group of environmental activists on a fund-raising binge: "international racket involving rare orchids . . . ruthless commercial exploitation and trafficking for profit" (*New Scientist*); "plundering rare orchids around the world" (*San Francisco Chronicle*); "Britain Imprisons an Orchid Pirate" (an Associated Press headline).

I began collecting the names of people who had been arrested or prosecuted for smuggling orchids. Henry Azadehdel, the plant collector that Richard had mentioned, was arrested at Heathrow Airport; the Indonesian grower Harto Kolopaking spent five months in the Lompoc federal prison in California; and Bosha Popow, a German grower, had his greenhouse raided by a government assault team armed with automatic weapons and attack dogs. Even the distinguished and highly respected French grower Marcel Lecoufle was battling a court case with customs officials and the World Wildlife Fund over his orchid collection. Intrigued by the media coverage and the use of potentially deadly force in the raid on Popow's greenhouse, I started searching for court records and other documents to find out more about the charges against these men. I also wondered what sort of person would smuggle an orchid; although I figured it would be next to impossible to track down these people and get them to talk, I was determined to try to find them.

The orchid publications in the library also yielded the names of dozens of people in the commercial orchid trade, and before long I was in regular communication with orchid growers, scientists, hobbyists, taxonomists, and botanical historians from New York, London, Hamburg, Amsterdam, Zürich, Paris, Copenhagen, the Isle of Jersey, Caracas, Mexico, Sikkim, and elsewhere. These initial contacts were soon followed by unexpected late-night telephone calls from mysterious people who wouldn't identify themselves. They all wanted to know why I was asking questions about the orchid trade, whom I was working for, and what I knew.

Clearly, what had seemed to me like the simple pursuit of amusing plant trivia was being interpreted as a potential threat by these people. The growers were cautious and some of them were afraid to talk to me about their business. "I've got three children to put through college with my orchids," a former Detroit policeman–turned–orchid grower pleaded. He agreed to talk, but only on the condition that I wouldn't use his name. I didn't understand the atmosphere of fear, but one contact eventually led to the next. Confidence and trust grew and before long I found myself spending nearly all of my time with the orchid people.

One of the first orchid growers I met was eighty-four-year-old Eleanor Kerrigan. Eleanor lives in a typical two-story older house on a quiet street in a suburb of Seattle, Washington. Seen from the sidewalk, there is nothing about the exterior of the building to suggest that her basement has been converted into a subterranean greenhouse that duplicates the temperature, light, air flow, and humidity of a tropical rain forest. Thousands of exotic orchids sway to an artificial jungle breeze in this hidden world filled with the sweet, mushroomy perfume of decomposing potting mix and healthy plants.

Eleanor has grown rare orchids at home for nearly forty years. At first she openly went about her business of tending to her collection, entering the plants in competitions, attending annual orchid symposiums, and infrequently advertising her plants for sale in trade publications. She was simply considered an enthusiastic hobbyist until around 1990, when a new and more restrictive set of CITES trade regulations went into effect with the inclusion of the entire genus *Paphiopedilum* in Appendix I. She told me that overnight, most of her orchids became "illegal" because she didn't have documentation to prove how long she had owned the plants or where they came from. This lack of paperwork made her just the sort of person that federal agents working for the U.S. Department of the Interior's Fish and Wildlife Service would like to get their hands on.

The morning I met Eleanor, large snowflakes fluttered past the kitchen window as we sat down for a mid-morning cup of tea. Outside, the gray sky cast a diffuse light on the rows of parked cars at curbside. Eleanor's hunched shoulders were draped with a peach-colored down comforter and Mr. Nibs, a large black-and-white cat, slept on her lap. On the breakfast table in front of her, Eleanor had arranged some of her orchid beauties for me, such as Magic Lantern, Heaven's Gate, and the White Knight. She explained that the parents of these orchid hybrids were plant species that had been wild-collected in Asia and imported in the 1980s when it was still possible to do so. But now if the Fish and Wildlife Service discovered these breeding plants in her basement greenhouse she could be subject to fines of tens of thousands of dollars, jail time, and the confiscation of her lifetime collection of orchids, worth $70,000. This sight of this old woman quietly sipping tea in her kitchen and enjoying the beauty of her orchids made for an unlikely-looking international crime scene.

"My lovely horticultural contraband. Oh, how I adore it." Eleanor sighed and looked out the window at the snow-covered street.

Eleanor breeds tropical lady's slipper orchids and she appreciates the blooms for what they are: the elaborate stage settings for the sex organs of her plants. From my side of the table the flowers were putting on a lascivious display with their gaudy colors, intoxicating scents, and glistening pink labial folds embellished with fine hairs and inviting orifices. According to Eleanor, the plants had been exuding strange smells and displaying their charms for a week in hopes of enticing some tropical insect to fondle their ripe pollen sacs. The stigma of one flower was cleverly camouflaged as a female moth in heat, but its nearest potential mate was half a world away in the mountain forests of Sikkim. Without the presence of natural insect pollinators, the plant's procreative function was dependent on Eleanor's deft strokes with a fine-haired brush or the tip of a wooden knitting needle that she had whittled to a delicate point.

"A bodice ripper!" Eleanor exclaimed as she gestured to Magic Lantern, a luscious, pink-purple hybrid of two Asian species, *Paphiopedilum micranthum* and *P. delenatii*.

"Bodice ripper?" I took a closer look at the flower. The shiny, candy-apple-red staminode that covered the reproductive organs was shaped like an extended tongue identical to the Rolling Stones logo. This shocking red protrusion nestled in the cleavage of two blushing petals then dropped down as if to lick the tip of an inverted pouch that looked like the head of an engorged penis. The blatant carnality of Magic Lantern was unmistakable and I found myself wondering what sort of impression the flower was making on the old woman.

"You don't have the eye yet, but it will come with time and experience," she laughed, assuming I didn't notice the erotic features of Magic Lantern. She handed me a copy of a wholesale orchid grower's catalogue to look at while she boiled more water for the teapot. I thumbed through the pages to familiarize myself with the range of flower forms. Immediately I was confronted with centerfolds showing downy, smooth petals and moistened, hot-pink lips that pouted in the direction of tautly curved shafts and heavily veined pouches. In contrast to the lascivious photos the captions seemed mundane and absurdly understated. They conveyed little more than taxonomic babble detailing tetraploid forms, wartlike structures, albinism, and petal morphology. The text and the lists of species and hybrids for sale did nothing for me, but I assumed that the cryptic passages and Latin binomials were more than enough to quicken the pulse beat and warm the loins of a true orchidophile.

We talked about orchid breeding and hybridizing for several hours, until it was time for Eleanor's afternoon nap. As I stood up to leave, the old woman caressed an orchid with a light touch of her fingertips and murmured, "Big, fat, full . . . and fabulous." I took one last look at the flower, which had a pair of elaborate wings and a hood attached to a brown-veined, shiny, scrotumlike pouch. This was *Paphiopedilum venustum*—the most obscene-looking flower of the lot.

Shortly after I met Eleanor the two of us attended the annual meeting of the Paphiopedilum Growers Guild, held in Shell Beach, California. The meeting was organized by eighty-eight-year-old Norris Powell. Norris, a legendary curmudgeon in the orchid world, is the owner of The Orchid House, located in the nearby town of Los Osos. For the last fifty years Norris has been a pioneering breeder of *Paphiopedilum* hybrids. He is greatly admired and feared for his flamboyant salesmanship and marketing techniques, but no one denies that he was instrumental in helping to transform the growing of rare orchids from a loose confederation of backyard hobbyists in the 1950s into a high-tech industry that is now part of an estimated $9 billion orchid business worldwide. Once everyone was seated in the conference hall, Norris delivered the opening speech.

"We come from all over the damn country!" Norris called out in a gruff voice. "From all over the whole world, I tell you! But you know what? We all speak the same language . . . we speak orchid, and that's why we're all here!"

The people in the audience nodded in approval, and with those words the conference was under way. Norris introduced the guest speakers and went on to warm up the crowd with announcements about the discovery of new species of slipper orchids, recent greenhouse raids, upcoming orchid shows, and new multifloral hybrids, followed by his least favorite subject: the latest round of CITES regulations to control the world trade in orchids.

"Imagine lawyers and bureaucrats tryin' to regulate an industry they don't know the first damn thing about! Hell, those experts get paid plenty to make us all miserable, but they can't even tell the difference between a dead herbarium specimen and a live plant. They don't want to regulate the orchid trade, they want to kill it! That's what they want to do. I'll tell ya, I'd like to kick some butt!" Norris concluded, before sitting down to raucous applause.

Following Paphiopedilum Guild meeting tradition, individuals stood up one-by-one to introduce themselves; and just as Norris had said, they came from everywhere: Japan, Venezuela, Russia, Germany, South Africa, Australia, Denmark, Taiwan, Great Britain, France, Brazil, Mexico, and every corner of the United States. With an assortment of names like Yuki Suzuki, Ernest Hetherington, Felix Saez de Ibarra, Harold Koopowitz, Leonid Averyanov, and Norman Fang in the crowd, I looked forward to mingling during the coffee breaks and in the evenings.

The three-day conference included numerous well-planned lectures about growing healthy plants, but the weekend was also part swap meet and orchid show, plus an opportunity for growers to broker deals and trade plants, pollen, and seed pods out in the parking lot. The brief intervals between lectures were filled with intense discussion and debate, followed by plenty of delicious gossip, back stabbing, drinking, and carousing at the karaoke bar in the Cliff's Hotel in the evening. What went on in the hotel rooms after dark between the orchid growers was any-one's guess.

At meals and during the mid-morning and afternoon breaks in the conference, I sat in on bewildering discussions about the fine points of orchid growing. Orchid lovers like Eleanor enjoy the solitude of working in their greenhouses, but when they get together they can talk for hours about chromosome counts, the taxonomy of the angraecoids of Madagascar and the cytological distinctions between the lip color intensities of *Paphiopedilum violascens* versus *P. bougainvilleanum*. They have strong opinions and can go toe-to-toe in heated debates over subjects like root tip anatomy, staminode architecture, nocturnal pollination strategies, sexual deceit, floral mimicry, insect pollinator fidelity, and spathulate leaf shapes. The more business-minded people simply wanted to snoop around to find out what new hybrids were selling well.

At one point during the proceedings, the taxonomist Eric Christiansen took me aside. "There are the orchid people and then there are the paphiopedilum people," he told me. "Don't get the two groups confused. The paph people are in a world of their own. They are known to be opinionated, unpredictable, and often dangerous, so be careful." I wasn't quite sure how to interpret this sort of information, but I thanked him for the warning.

After the first day of the meeting the numbing orchid chatter was beginning to sound like the ravings of horticultural insiders who could no longer appreciate the simple beauty of a flower or recognize the unmistakable sensuality of the blooms. But on the last day of the conference Randy Wayne-Thruste, a black-leather-motorcycle-jacketed orchid grower, judge, and consultant for several private orchid collections in Florida, gave a slide presentation of award-winning orchids from the previous year. He looked like Charles Manson, and the previous night at the karaoke bar nasty rumors circulated about how Randy had built up his breeding stock by dividing or pilfering prize plants from his clients—mostly elderly growers who could no longer keep track of what they had in their greenhouses. A Christian orchid breeder (who didn't believe in the theory of evolution) told me that Randy was in the habit of French-kissing his English bull-dog as a way of testing the mettle of new visitors to his green-house.

Eleanor sat next to me during the presentation. When the lights had dimmed in the conference room and the first few slides had been projected, I became aware of movement in the audience. All around me people were shifting discreetly in their chairs and I could sense a change in mood.

Each slide was illuminated on the screen just long enough for Randy to identify the flower, mention the award and score given by the American Orchid Society judges, and then name the grower. People's eager faces were dimly illuminated while each image was projected, and between slides the darkened lecture hall was filled with the sounds of excited whispers.

"Hummph!" snorted Eleanor in response to several new hybrids that were not to her liking.

"*Paphiopedilum glaucophyllum*, variety *moquettianum*," Randy announced grandly, and immediately the room rumbled with murmurs of pleasure. The sounds of floral adoration con-tinued to build in intensity, and as the slide show progressed the room grew warmer and I thought I could detect the sound of heavy breathing nearby. Randy introduced each flower in a pre-cise, reverential manner, with just the right touch of arrogance and ostentation to make the presentation very enjoyable. But I found it difficult to concentrate on the beautiful flowers with their exotic-sounding names and subtle variations of color and form, because I kept thinking about what it would be like to French-kiss a bulldog.

Randy continued his roll call of award winners. As the audience warmed to the gorgeous slides, he responded to their mood by modulating his voice into a coy, cooing delivery. By this time the flowers had worked their magic and the audience started making the sorts of stifled moans and grunts that are more frequently associated with the midday crowd at an adult movie house.

"Mmmmmm . . . luscious . . . ," someone gasped nearby.

One slide showed a large vini-colored *Paphiopedilum* Maudiae-type hybrid. "Now that . . . is one . . . fat . . . flower!" proclaimed Randy, calling out the parentage like some sort of orchid preacher at a plant revival meeting.

"Wow . . . Big Red!" came a response from the darkness.

"I'm in love!" cried out a woman.

"I'll take it," declared an elderly male voice from somewhere in the back.

"Rare, unusual . . . and exceedingly ugly," Eleanor muttered quietly, as she fidgeted in her seat.

This celebration of the flowers went on for nearly an hour and a half before the house lights came up and I looked around at the dreamy, knowing expressions on the faces of the orchid people. Eleanor, obviously disgusted by the grotesque and unnatural-looking features of several of the new hybrids, immediately headed off in the direction of the hotel bar.

During the lunch break, I sat with Joe Kunisch, an intense, compact man with a penetrating stare and a carefully trimmed mustache. Joe is a highly regarded grower who owns Bloomfield

Orchids in upstate New York. He told me how his interest in orchids had started with a single plant on the windowsill of his kitchen thirty-five years earlier.

"I used to own a large plastic injection molding company in Rochester," he explained. "We made auto parts, and all sorts of other products for Kodak and Xerox. Then I bought a cattleya hybrid at an orchid show. It didn't take long before I killed it, but that was how it all started. Pretty soon I decided I wanted another orchid. First a red one, then a pink one, then I had to have a white one with spots. Before long, the windowsill and kitchen table were covered with the things. I started to grow orchids in the basement under mercury vapor lamps. My wife thought I was nuts, but I kept adding to my collection. I couldn't stop. Orchid growing was my hobby for twenty-five years, so when I got tired of injection-molded plastic about ten years ago I knew exactly what I wanted to do. Now I have a 2,200-square-foot greenhouse with about 200,000 plants. I sold the plastic business to finance the orchids and now all I do is grow and sell orchids. A lot of growers just see orchids as a way to make money, but I still bring my favorite plants into the house when they are in bloom so that I can enjoy the flowers. My life completely revolves around tending to my orchids."

"Well, at least you have plenty of fellow orchid lovers to share your interest with here," I said, glancing around the room.

Without taking his eyes off me, he leaned forward. "You know, the only people that are weirder than us are the dog show people . . . and we are not a distant second by any means."

Joe nervously lit a cigarette and started talking with a man from Kansas City who was seated across the table. The man, who had spent far too much time styling and blow-drying his hair, had been into sanitary engineering before he discovered orchid breeding. He explained how he was planning to market himself as a dream maker, a magician of color and form who created beautiful flowers. He then went on to tell us how his first wife couldn't deal with his orchid obsession. One morning she sat him down at the breakfast table and explained that he would have to choose between his orchid collection and their marriage.

"That's the easiest decision I'll ever make," he told her. "You're out of here, baby!"

The discussion shifted to a raunchy joke about *Cypripedium acaule* and the origin of the name *Cypripedium*. The word is derived from the Greek *Kypris pedion*, which translates as "the genital region of Aphrodite." One look at the wrinkled, pink, pouting, vertical lips of *Cypripedium acaule* explains it all. Then the orchid people discussed the merits of a product called Plant Shine.

"What is Plant Shine?" I asked.

"Like the stuff they put on body builders and porn stars," said Joe. "It makes the leaves glisten."

"Oh," I mumbled.

A third man seated at the table described a fellow grower in Santa Barbara who wore camouflaged army fatigues in the greenhouse and carried an Uzi submachine gun while tending his plants. A large man with fleshy lips told me that if I licked the mealy-coated callus of *Maxillaria huebschii*, my tongue would go numb. I didn't bother asking him how he had made this unusual discovery, or what a mealy-coated callus might be, because after three days with the orchid people I knew it was time to be around normal human beings for a while.

I thanked Norris for his kind invitation to attend the orchid growers' symposium, and then drove north to spend the night with friends in a house perched high on a ridge of the Santa Lucia Mountains. We had dinner overlooking the moonlit Big Sur coast while far below us car headlights cut into the night as they silently wound their way up and down the coast highway. A log fire crackled in the fireplace and the wine was uncorked as powerful gusts of wind rattled the windowpanes and bumped against the doors. My host and hostess anticipated an evening filled with stories about beautiful flowers and the fine art of orchid breeding, but all they heard were strange tales of midnight greenhouse break-ins with chain saws, orchid smuggling routes, "safe houses," thefts of award-winning plants from orchid shows, government sting operations, orchid licking, fraud, murder, and money.

"It sounds like the illegal drug trade," they laughed.

"I think it might be worse," I said.

Chapter 3

THE WIZARD OF OZ

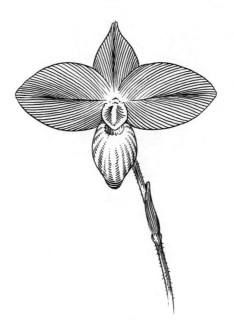

Pragmipedium besseae Eat My Dust

I had several hours to spare the following morning, so I decided to visit an orchid grower whom Eleanor called the Wizard of OZ. His nursery was only a short distance off the coast road. Eleanor had given me the man's phone number during the orchid conference. I called ahead to make sure the place was open and to get detailed directions to the nursery.

Carefully hidden away at the end of a confusion of country lanes, in the rolling hills near Watsonville, California, is the Orchid Zone, a 77,000-square-foot greenhouse complex that is home to more than a million rare and exotic orchids. Walking into OZ, as it is known in the orchid world, is like entering a Ray Bradbury story. Each greenhouse runs on a high-tech life-support system that controls light, heat, cooling, and humidity by computer. Three-foot-wide tubes of clear perforated plastic run overhead, wafting a tropical breeze over a colorful sea of bobbing flowers. Up near the roof, fabric curtains, on sliding metal tracks, open to compensate for the shadows of passing clouds. Automatic misters come on without warning and a fresh, earthy smell of compost and potting mix permeates the damp air.

Seated on a chair, in a special area known as the Stud Room, I found Terry Root, a bearded, 250-pound, cigar-smoking, beer-drinking, kick-ass biker with a ponytail who breeds exotic orchids for a living. Terry owns and manages the Orchid Zone, and when I arrived he was preparing to pollinate a tray full of rare slipper orchids with a toothpick. Terry's plants are famous for their spectacular form, color range, and bizarre markings, and the Orchid Zone has a reputation for growing the finest, most unusual slipper orchid hybrids in the world. Slipper orchid breeders are attracted to the peculiar and the obscene, and even a cursory glance at their work makes it clear that kinky black hairs, warts, spots, veins, glistening pouches, luscious pink folds, and erect columns are what the hybridizers dream of.

"Orchid breeding?" Terry remarked as he closely examined the first flower. "It's an illness, an addiction. The species purists say it's unnatural, this practice of cross-pollinating orchids, but in the end that's what it takes to create something unique and beautiful."

Terry's fists looked like they were capable of driving railroad spikes, but as he delicately transferred pollen from one orchid to the other with a gentle caress of his toothpick, the biker image fell away and I began to understand why he is known as the Wizard of OZ.

Unlike most orchids, slipper orchids can't yet be propagated by tissue culture, which is why Terry has to hand-pollinate each flower. Once the seed pod is mature, it is cut open and the dust-like orchid seeds are placed in sterile flasks containing a special gel-like growth medium. The young seedlings develop in this sterile environment until they are large enough to be planted in flats. The flats are placed in a nursery and the seedlings continue to grow until they are divided and potted up into individual containers.

Exotic flower forms are what drive the hybrid orchid business, and hybrids are a unique act of creation that reflects the breeder's individual style. The process is partially technique but mostly art, and with a lead time of anywhere from six to eighteen years to get from seed to finished flower, the slipper orchid game is all about capital investment, anticipation, vision, bluster, and blind faith. Terry has never been in the jungle where the orchids grow, but through observation and trial and error he knows what makes the plants thrive. According to Terry, the secret to growing healthy orchids is the complete avoidance of stress on the plants. This means maintaining a delicate balance of water, light, nutrients, temperature, humidity, and air flow.

"When it comes to pollinating, we like to think we do a better job than the bugs in the jungle," Terry said. He reeled off the names of some of his favorite Orchid Zone creations. There was Screaming Eagle, Ruby Slippers, Cyberspace, Flasher, Big Mama, 180 Proof, Jail Bait, Rolling Thunder, and my favorite, Eat My Dust—a tribute to Terry's biker heart. Surrounded by thousands of beautiful plants, Terry explained that the Orchid Zone is a high-end wholesale outlet that caters to an exclusive group of buyers. Clients come from Japan, Australia, Taiwan, South America, Europe, Mexico, Canada, even Alaska. A Buddhist monk from Thailand, dressed in saffron robes, walked in one day looking for a rare albino form of a particular species of orchid. Next to impossible to find in the wild, but Terry had the plant. A Taiwanese client bought one of Terry's hybrids off the bench for $20,000, but many of the Orchid Zone's mature, pedigreed breeding plants are not for sale at any price. High-end clients have been known to spend $75,000 on a single buying trip.

"In the seventeenth century, tulip mania swept Europe," Terry told me. "Fortunes were lost speculating on rare bulbs, and now it's orchid fever that's on the rampage. But this is nothing new. Plants go in and out of fashion all the time. The same sort of hybridizing frenzy happened with hyacinths, daffodils, roses, and camellias."

The Orchid Zone produces 10,000 artificially propagated seedlings per month, but barely keeps up with demand. Most of its business comes by word of mouth—a remarkable achievement in the high-stakes, petty, cutthroat world of orchid growing, where breeding programs are kept top secret and armed guards and attack dogs patrol many nurseries. Other orchid growers produce lavishly illustrated color catalogues to tantalize customers, but Terry has learned that in the orchid business nothing sells like consistency, innovation, and healthy, dependable plants. Buyers' appetites for new hybrids are insatiable, so Terry likes to cover his bets by producing around 2,000 new hybrids each year.

"Mistakes are part of the learning process," Terry explained, "and from time to time we produce some really ugly flowers."

After Terry had finished pollinating his orchids he showed me around the property. He is not the sort of man who understands the concept of leisure time, and when he is not looking after his thirty employees or his orchids, he breeds emus, peacocks, and countless numbers of Chinese carp. Several hundred-gallon saltwater tanks are built into the walls of his living room for his tropical fish collection and what was once the breakfast room is now filled with terrariums that house land tortoises, iguanas, and other reptiles. The day of my visit, dozens of long, slithering bodies with scales and tails and scratchy claws were trying to climb out of the terrariums.

"Terry likes to grow things," explained his diminutive wife.

On a low hill in the middle of the Orchid Zone's complex of greenhouses, a winding yellow brick pathway leads to a white-domed private observatory where Terry keeps track of solar eruptions with a sixteen-inch telescope. A computerized tracking device helps him to study a theory that sunspots affect the growth of orchids.

Terry took me into his laboratory where row after row of shelves were filled with sterile containers that held more than 500,000 orchid seedlings. With a state-of-the-art, high-tech artificial propagation laboratory like this one, I assumed that the government authorities would take no interest in the Orchid Zone. But this has not been the case. In the late 1980s an informer told British customs officials that the Orchid Zone was part of an international network smuggling rare wild-collected plants. The phone at OZ was tapped for several months, then Terry received a visit from special agent Larry Farrington of the U.S. Department of the Interior. He was accompanied by two British customs agents.

"Up until then, it was cute, this orchid pirate idea," Terry told me. "We kind of laughed about it until the day the customs people turned up at the front door. They showed us a file of wire-tapped telephone conversations that I had with the orchid hunter Henry Azadehdel, and I'll tell you that scared the hell out of us. We were squeaky-clean before they showed up, but I'll tell you, we got even more squeaky-clean after they left."

The investigation was the result of Terry's having bought five *Paphiopedilum sanderianum* plants from Ray Rands, a southern California orchid dealer, in 1985. These plants had been brought into the United States by Henry Azadehdel. The Orchid Zone wanted to introduce the sanderianum into its breeding program. One of the plants died, but Terry managed to flower the rest and get seed pods from the remaining plants. From these four originals—Deep Pockets, Jacob's Ladder, Daddy Long Legs, and Deep Flight—the Orchid Zone has propagated nearly

5,000 healthy plants. In less than ten years Terry may have produced more sanderianum plants than exist in the wild. He paid
around $3,500 each for the original breeding plants, but now
with large numbers of sanderianums coming on line he can sell
their offspring for about $250 each.

"At those prices who in their right mind is going to go climbing around in the jungle busting their ass to collect wild plants?
No one. And this helps to take the pressure off the wild population," Terry said. "To some people our breeding program is all
part of an evil orchid-smuggling conspiracy. To any intelligent
person this sort of activity is called conservation."

By mid-afternoon OZ had closed down for the day and Terry
was tired of talking orchid politics. He wanted to show me his
motorcycles and the six-foot-tall incubating cabinet for emu
eggs that he had just finished. Then it was time for the beer, the
cigars, the telescope, and finally dinner. Fourteen hours after
arriving at the Orchid Zone I returned to the coast highway and
headed back to San Francisco in the dark.

Chapter 4

ORCHID FEVER

Cattleya labiata

I have a letter from Norway that I keep pinned to the wall of my office. The letter arrived several years ago, but from time to time I read it to recapture a sense of what orchids can do to the lives of normal people. The letter reads:

Dear Sir,

I am writing to you from the village of Nordkjosbotn, which is on the road between Narvik and Tromso. We are just above the Arctic Circle about 70 degrees north latitude on the southern edge of the Barents Sea. If you look at a map you will notice that we are quite a bit north of Iceland. A friend in the Norwegian Orchid Society told me that you are looking for people who grow tropical orchids in unusual places.

I do not know if the climate here is extreme enough for your purpose, but here is my story. I live with my family which includes 420 tropical orchids. I grow my orchids together with melons and tomatoes in a small greenhouse from March until October and the rest of the time the orchids are put in the laundry room under lights where they stay warm for the winter months. My wife thinks that the orchids have taken over my life. She calls them my "green harlots." This is probably true, but I remind her that, despite the orchids, I have found enough spare time and energy to help produce and raise two children with her and that we are still married. The expense of keeping my orchids alive and happy in Nordkjosbotn protects me from spending money on unhealthy activities that my friends pursue during the long winter months, and for this my wife should be glad.

That is what I can tell you. You are welcome to come visit Nordkjosbotn and see my orchid collection, but try to come during the months when we have sun light.

Sincerely,

Thorkild Sven Janson

I had promptly written back to Mr. Janson, thanking him for his letter and the invitation to visit, but I regretfully informed him that due to prior work commitments I would be unable to visit Nordkjosbotn in the foreseeable future. The truth of the matter was that his letter gave me such a clear vision of what it must be like to keep orchids in Norway that I felt absolutely no need to go look at his greenhouse/laundry room setup. To this day I have a vision of him tending his tropical orchids, in the dead of winter, by the feeble light of the aurora borealis. Whenever I think of Mr. Janson I wonder about the effort and expense that must go into the upkeep of tropical orchids north of the Arctic Circle, and why anyone would be inclined to attempt such a feat. Mr. Janson's letter, and many others like it that I had solicited from around the world, suggested a vast and far-flung horticultural cult, the size of which I could only guess at.

For more than a year I followed dozens of leads that took me on short and often very strange journeys into the orchid world. Stories of questionable origin circulated about how private jets, stuffed with rare orchids, flew high-rolling orchid lovers in and out of countries where the local farmers were raking the same orchids into piles and feeding them to their pigs. As implausible as these and other stories sounded, the orchid people I began to meet soon gave me plenty of reasons to suspend my disbelief.

I met Bob Welts, a flamboyant former New York commodities broker who now lives in Santa Barbara, California. He is a wildly successful, award-winning orchid grower who drives a white Rolls Royce. For years he has run his business from his greenhouse with a fax machine and a laptop computer. According to one of his friends, he once made $65,000 in a one-hour trading session, then turned to his orchids, rubbed his hands gleefully, and with a smile announced, "That's enough for one day. Now back to my babies!"

Orchids are also the passion of Hiroshi Ikarashi, a reclusive Japanese real estate developer with dozens of commercial properties in the central business district of Kobe. He responded to the devastating early morning earthquake in 1994 by rushing naked from his demolished home to check the orchids in the greenhouse. "Thanks to God," he told me, "the greenhouse all broken, but plants only knocked on their side. I tell you, I am astonish. But then I begin to wonder: Where my wife in the rubble of our house?"

Even today, tantalizing tips (along with a surprising amount of salacious gossip) about people in the orchid world continue to arrive by phone, fax, and e-mail. I've heard that Dr. Phyllis Nibbler of the Bethnal Green Horticultural Society in London was charged by a rhinoceros while she was bent over inspecting an orchid in Africa. The person who told me the story claimed that it was the sound of thundering hooves and the vibrating ground beneath her feet that alerted her to the danger. I have since learned from Dr. Nibbler that the story has been greatly exaggerated, but I still cherish my image of a gray-haired and bespectacled middle-aged British orchidophile clinging to a fragile orchid flower after having been flattened by a charging rhinoceros.

My friend Manfred Waffender, a filmmaker from Frankfurt, told me that Khun Sa, the head of the renegade Wa Army in the Shan State of Burma, was an orchid fancier. The eastern edge of Shan State, where it borders Yunnan Province in China, contains some of the most dazzling orchid habitats on earth, so when two clandestine bio-prospectors from a German pharmaceutical company gave me the phone number of a person who could take me into Burma from northern Thailand, I contacted the man immediately. I made plans to rendezvous with him in Chiang Mai; only a last-minute outbreak of fighting in Burma in 1996 prevented me from doing so. I had little interest in entering a battle zone to discuss rare orchids, and I was also quite certain that Khun Sa would be preoccupied with commanding his troops.

Instead of going to Burma to talk about orchids with the warlord Khun Sa, I flew to New York City to talk with Harry Zelenko. Mr. Zelenko is the founder of Zelenko Associates, a graphics, advertising, and industrial design firm. Harry also grows orchids. He is an accomplished watercolorist and he lives with his wife in a tastefully restored brownstone on the Upper East Side of Manhattan. On the roof of their six-story building is a nineteen-by-thirty-two-foot greenhouse filled with approximately 2,500 orchids, including oncidiums, cochleanthes, phragmipediums, cattleyas, encyclias, catasetums, and laelias, with many other genera tucked away on the multitiered nursery benches. The day I arrived snow flurries were swirling across the rooftops and the greenhouse was blanketed with white.

Oncidium orchids are Harry's thing, and during the eleven years prior to my visit he had been painting watercolors of the different *Oncidium* species in his collection in hopes of producing a large folio book on the entire genus. When he first started the project, sometime around 1985, he thought that there were less than 200 species of oncidiums. Before long, he discovered that the number was closer to 600. He kept acquiring plants, flowering them, and producing paintings until he received a bit of sobering news from Dr. Mark Chase, a specialist in oncidiums, who at the time was the head of the Laboratory of Molecular Systematics at the Royal Botanic Gardens, Kew. Dr. Chase informed Harry that the Oncidium Alliance also included *Odontoglossum, Brassia, Miltonia, Sigmotastalix,* and other genera, which meant that the plants to be collected, flowered, and painted now numbered more than 1,200 species.

Harry claims that he took the news well, but one suspects that he was beginning to tire of the irksome process and expense of locating and importing the necessary plants. The time-consuming delays involved with obtaining the proper CITES documents and phytosanitary permits for the plants had clearly become irksome, as Harry's life was reduced (or elevated, depending on how you feel about orchids) to concentrating on a monumental painting project that had no end in sight. By the time I met him, he had painted more than 900 species. His design business was put on hold, and both he and his wife were spending a good deal of their time researching, growing, and painting orchids. But there are limits to this sort of obsession; Harry told me if Dr. Chase or some other scientist had the nerve to add further to the number of species, he didn't want to know about it. As far as Harry was concerned, the nomenclatural nit-pickers could do as they liked, but he was drawing the line at 1,200 species.

The skies darkened and large snowflakes were coming down as we entered the damp tropical heat of his rooftop greenhouse. Surrounded by his collection of orchids, Harry described the structure as "an attic for an addict." As I stepped outside the greenhouse for a few moments, I could just make out the familiar neighborhood landmarks through the falling snow: the Citicorp Building, the Chrysler Building, and the upper structure of the 59th Street Bridge. Back in the greenhouse, the gas heaters switched off and automatic misters sprang to life, raising the humidity to ideal tropical conditions.

"*Telundia scandens*," Harry called out, as I paused to examine one of his oncidiums. "A Cuban orchid," he muttered. "I waited ten years for that sucker to flower."

Oscillating fans bathed us in a warm, damp mist as Harry removed a rubber-tipped dental tool from his shirt pocket and started searching his precious plants for mealybugs and scale. With his eyeglasses fogged from the humidity, Harry tried to explain his obsession with orchids.

"Well, I know it started with a three-dollar orchid that I bought out of a catalogue in 1962, but after that it's unclear how a simple weekend hobby could have led to this. These plants own my life. I am their willing prisoner, and I often find myself talking to them, nurturing them, and praying for them to bloom."

When I asked Harry where he found his plants, he told me that orchid growers, scientists, and collectors from around the world sent him species that he was looking for. Some orchids arrived on loan, but most of them were purchased or obtained through trade. I was curious to know if he was having any difficulty importing these orchids.

"Look, this may be difficult for you to understand," Harry explained, "but there are people, and I'm not going to mention any names, who would like to annihilate someone like me for collecting and painting orchids. These are the sorts of people who lose sleep fretting about some fucking salamander living in a cave, but when it comes to stopping the orchid habitats of the world from being bulldozed and burned to the ground, they just look the other way and say they are only concerned about the effect of illegal trade on endangered species."

For orchid lovers like Harry, cave-dwelling salamanders are rated only slightly higher than mealybugs, fungus gnats, and spider mites. Clearly, he had entered one of the advanced stages of orchid fever. The seasons come and go, but on most days Harry can be found at his easel, paintbrush and magnifying glass in hand, utterly intoxicated by the heavenly sight of a well-flowered oncidium.

After my visit with Harry in New York, I began to develop a friendship with the Venezuelan orchid grower Felix Saez de Ibarra. I originally met Felix at Norris Powell's annual orchid meeting in southern California. At the time I quickly realized that Felix was the sort of elegant, cultured, hand-kissing Latin American gentleman-scholar that has all but vanished from modern society. He operates one of the largest cement manufacturing facilities in Caracas, but over the years of our correspondence and friendship I have constantly been astonished by his sense of grace and the ease with which he moves in the world. I once took Felix and a group of friends to Borneo, where I saw him take his wife in his arms and dance a perfectly executed merengue (without music) in the middle of the rain forest for the enjoyment of a group of indigenous people dressed in loincloths and holding spears. What made this performance even more impressive was the fact that two days earlier, while climbing a nearly vertical limestone cliff in search of *Paphiopedilum stonei,* he had split open a kneecap on the razor-sharp rocks. Most people would have flown home for emergency medical treatment, but instead, Felix bandaged his knee and danced beneath the moon with a head full of music and orchid dreams.

Felix's love of Latin-Caribbean music, salsa dancing, and conversation is only equaled by his passion for exotic Venezuelan orchids. Over the years, Felix has been known to climb into his private plane and, on a whim, risk his life by flying to remote, grassy landing strips at the headwaters of the Orinoco River for the sole purpose of studying how these orchids grow in the wild. For more than ten years he has made repeated trips to collect rain and river water and leaf and soil samples from the habitat of *Phragmipedium klotzscheanum*. Few people have been successful in keeping this plant alive for more than a few years, and it is one of Felix's dreams to unlock the cultural secrets of this mysterious and beautifully flowered slipper orchid.

But when it comes to orchid collecting in the late twentieth century, there are few botanical quests that measure up to those taken by the Dunstervilles in the Gran Sabana region of Venezuela. Galfrid Clement Keyworth Dunsterville was born to British parents in India shortly before World War I. He trained as a petroleum engineer, married, and eventually settled in Caracas as the president of Shell Oil Company. During one of the many orchid-collecting trips the Dunstervilles made in preparation for their definitive six-volume *Venezuelan Orchids Illustrated,* Galfrid and his wife, the intrepid Nora, climbed the remote and forbidding Auyán Tepui, a 5,000-foot-high sandstone plateau that towers above the jungle, near the headwaters of the Río Carrao. Reading Dunsterville's account of that 1963 journey will give you a fair idea of what orchid fever can do to a civilized human being.

A five-day approach on foot, through clouds of biting insects, with a string of local porters, brought them to the foot of the plateau. Then, savaged by ticks, they proceeded to claw their way to the top in two days. Once they reached the rim of the plateau, they stumbled through the wild and broken jungle terrain for the better part of two weeks in search of drinking water, flat places to pitch their tent, and new species of orchids such as *Sobralia infundibuligiera, Elleanthus norae,* and the diminutive *Pinelia alticola.* At one point, Nora disappeared with a scream when she fell through the false floor of the jungle. She was rescued from a narrow ledge overlooking a fetid abyss. Then one night during the harrowing descent from the plateau, the entire orchid collection was attacked and partially destroyed by a migrating army of leaf-cutting ants. At journey's end, Nora attained cult status among orchid hunters with her memorable description of bathing in a stagnant jungle sinkhole, lined with mud and smelling of fresh tapir dung.

From my own journey to Fire Mountain in search of *Paphiopedilum sanderianum,* I knew the weirdly electrifying thrill of discovering a rare orchid in bloom in the jungle. But this temporary surge of adrenaline hardly explained why people like Dr. Phyllis Nibbler would risk death by charging rhinoceros for the sake of a flower, or why Felix Saez would embark on flights over the Venezuelan rain forest in foul weather to collect orchid leaf tips and water samples for further study. And what would prompt a young woman such as Nora Dunsterville to subject herself to such indignities in the name of orchid research? Money seemed to have little if anything to do with these pursuits. The more people I talked to, the more mystified I became by the power of orchids to attract and then manipulate people into taking care of them. Orchid fever was clearly the most plausible explanation for such peculiar behavior.

The astonishing, dreamlike beauty of a well-flowered orchid is enough to captivate most people, but as with many other botanical pursuits, it is the quest for big meanings in little things that keeps the orchid growers, hobbyists, and scientists enchanted. The cultivation and breeding of orchids also exposes people to the challenges that arise when human expectations meet the inflexible rules of nature. With the possible exceptions of rosarians and tulip lovers, nowhere else in the plant world will you find so many individuals as devoted and passionate about flowers as the orchid people.

The worldwide retail orchid business is conservatively estimated at $9 billion annually. Thailand alone exports at least $250 million worth of orchids each year, and there are individual commercial growers in the United States that turn over $15 million each, in wholesale trade, year after year. Some 400,000 hobbyists who own collections valued at over $500 live in the United States, and 200 U.S. orchid suppliers are struggling to provide plants for a wholesale trade that by 1997 had already reached 8.5 million plants worth more than $64 million. This roughly translates into $150 million at the retail level, but these dollar amounts are little more than small change when compared to the European orchid nursery industry. Floricultura, the gigantic Dutch nursery located near Amsterdam, produces approximately 18 million orchids per year; delivery trucks fill its loading docks six days a week, ten hours a day. Based on increasing sales figures recorded by the U.S. Department of Agriculture, there is no end in sight to the burgeoning market as orchids rapidly become the current gardening passion. Several million people worldwide now grow orchids, and this botanical craze has already eclipsed both the nineteenth-century Victorian frenzy for orchids as well as the tulip madness that gripped the Netherlands in the seventeenth century.

Many people are under the impression that all orchids grow in tropical areas, but the orchid family is incredibly diverse and highly specialized. These plants have adapted over millions of years to many climates and habitats and are found on every continent except Antarctica. Orchids that grow on rock surfaces are known as lithophytes, orchids found on trees are epiphytes, and those that live in the ground are known as terrestrials.

Orchids represent one of the largest families of flowering plants. There are approximately 25,000 naturally occurring species and more than 100,000 artificial hybrids in cultivation. As a general rule, orchid flowers have three petals and three sepals, with both sex organs situated on the same column. Plants range in size from the microscopic Venezuelan orchid *Platystele ornata* (a bouquet of its flowers will fit on the head of a pin) to the Borneo giant, *Grammatophyllum speciosum*, which can weigh more than half a ton and measure forty feet in circumference. This monster of an orchid is often found growing as an epiphyte high above the ground on rain forest trees, and more than one collector has been maimed or crushed to death on the jungle floor while trying to dislodge this particular species.

More than any other plant under cultivation, orchids have captured the passions of both growers and scientists. Botanists have spent their careers exploring how these flowers manipulate, connive, court, and cheat insects into having sex with them. To attract specific insects, the flowers mimic moths, wasps, and bees, and many curious evolutionary developments have resulted from these strange partnerships between orchids and insects. In Madagascar, for example, *Angraecum sesquipedale* (also known as the Star of Bethlehem orchid) can be pollinated by only one species of night-flying moth, which, over time, has evolved a twelve-inch-long tongue that enables it to reach the nectar at the bottom of the flower's long nectary. While the moth is sipping nectar it receives a dusting of pollen on its forehead that will be transported to the next blossom. The male flower of the South American orchid *Catasetum denticulatum* doesn't waste time rewarding its pollinator with nectar or fragrant false promises. It simply waits for a bee to land on its lip, then fires a miniature, winged pollen dart from overhead. A quick-drying glue adheres the dart to the bee's back, where it will remain until the bee finds its way to the stigma of a different flower and completes its pollinating task.

Perhaps my favorite pollinating strategy is performed by *Drakaea livida,* the hammer orchid of Western Australia. Its pollinating insect, a male wasp, is attracted to the flower by a floral scent that bears an uncanny resemblance to the fragrance emitted by a female wasp that is badly in need of some companionship. The male wasp lands on the hairy lip of the flower and then rubs his tummy on its surface to determine if it is a suitable mate. All is well until the male grasps the lip and tries to take off for a bit of midair copulation. The lifting motion triggers a hinged device that repeatedly hammers the wasp between the lip and the column. During this process, pollen is either attached to the wasp or deposited on the flower, and only then is the wasp allowed to escape this rough treatment.

Regardless of whether the insects are beaten senseless with floral hammers or shot with sticky darts, they are free to go once they have assisted in the transfer of pollen. But human beings attracted to orchids do not get off quite so easily. Once a person has been properly seduced by the sight or scent of an orchid, he or she has little choice but to collect or buy the plant, take it home, build a special enclosure for it, feed, water, and groom the thing, and then dote over the plant for years. These people usually park their cars on the street because their garages are filled to capacity with potting tables surrounded with commercial quantities of cork bark, oyster shell, crushed dolomite, sphagnum moss, twist ties, horticultural charcoal, several different types of fertilizers, insecticides, pots, baskets, respirators, protective rubber clothing, perlite, tree ferns, and gardening stakes. These orchid people are referred to as hobbyists, but they cater to the needs of their beloved orchids with a single-minded devotion that blurs the line between love and lunacy.

With thousands of orchids to study, hybridize, clone, and breed, it is not surprising how much money and time some orchid people will invest to satisfy their passion for these unusual plants. Power, prestige, and profit are among the more mundane reasons people get involved with orchids. There is a certain cachet involved with owning something rare and beautiful, but curiosity, the love of exotic plants, the desire to create new hybrids, and the drive to uncover complex botanical mysteries are the prime incentives that attract and hold the interest of true orchid lovers. The American Orchid Society has approximately 30,000 members, and it is estimated that there are 4–5 million serious orchid hobbyists worldwide. These people share the common desire to cultivate something exquisite, unique, and beautiful, and their passion has created countless numbers of fragile, multiscented, living architectural wonders that reside in millions of five-inch pots perched on the back porches, breakfast tables, and windowsills of the world.

The origins of orchid fever can be traced back to ancient China. According to legend, in 2800 B.C. *Bletilla hyacinthiana* was mentioned by the Emperor Shen Nung in *Sheng Nung Pen Ts'ao Ching,* his book about the medicinal uses of plant and animal parts. The warrior/philosopher Confucius (551–479 B.C.) called the orchid "the king of fragrant plants," and by the tenth century a scholar by the name of Kin-sho had written *Orchid Book,* which provided names of cymbidium growers, areas where the plants grew in the wild, as well as cultural information and advice on which varieties to grow. The popularity of fragrant orchids eventually spread to Japan, and by the early seventeenth century members of the Japanese royalty were perfuming their clothes with *Dendrobium moniliforme.* Samurai, when they weren't hacking off the limbs of their opponents, sipping green tea, or reciting poetry, cultivated *Neofinetia falcata.* Wealthy merchants and other upper-class Japanese grew fragrant cymbidium species for their exquisite scent and variegated foliage.

The era of European colonial expansion greatly accelerated the collection of orchid plants and parts of plants from around the world. In the early sixteenth century dried seed pods from the vanilla orchid, *Vanilla planifolia,* were shipped from Mexico to Spain as a perfume and a flavoring for hot chocolate. The Dutch East India Company collected orchid specimens from India, Japan, Java, and the Spice Islands, and Jesuit missionaries, traders, and even people such as Captain William Bligh, Captain James Cook, and Sir Francis Drake collected orchids. Until the middle of the nineteenth century large numbers of orchid tubers were imported from Turkey to England for use in a hot milky drink called "saloop," which predated the wide use of coffee by the working class.

Among the earliest orchids cultivated in Europe was *Cypripedium acaule,* a North American terrestrial orchid that British colonists and merchants sent back to England. But not until 1818 was the stage set for orchid fever to explode on the British horticultural scene. In that year, according to orchid lore, Mr. William Swainson, a plant hunter who was working in Brazil, collected a number of unremarkable plants to be used as packing material for a shipment of other exotic specimens. When the crates arrived in England, William Cattley, who was interested in tropical plants, decided to try flowering a bit of Swainson's packing material. Toward the end of 1818 a number of huge and outrageously beautiful flowers were produced by this exceedingly ugly plant. These first flowers turned the British orchid world upside down, and John Lindley, who later became known as the father of modern orchidology, wrote a scientific description of the plant and named it *Cattleya labiata,* in honor of Cattley.

Not long after the discovery of *Cattleya labiata,* the craze for exotic tropical orchids began to take its toll on the British aristocracy. In 1826 William Spencer Cavendish, the sixth duke of Devonshire, laid eyes on *Oncidium papilio* and, according to his contemporaries, the man was never quite the same again. He had Joseph Paxton, his head gardener, design a greenhouse that measured approximately 300 feet long, 150 feet wide, and 35 feet tall. Within this massive structure, the duke pursued his orchid hobby with a degree of fanaticism that marked him for life. Even during the height of the Victorian orchid frenzy, no one could touch the duke of Devonshire when it came to spending vast sums of money on their collections of exotic orchids.

It wasn't long before commercial nurseries and their networks of professional orchid hunters were searching the most distant corners of the world for new and unusual species to satisfy the rapidly increasing number of affluent orchid growers.

At this time, botanical institutions, private collectors, and commercial growers were totally dependent on one another. They exchanged plants and cultural information in a way that accelerated scientific study, improved greenhouse design, and disseminated horticultural knowledge. Auctions and retail sales of orchids also benefited the great orchid nurseries such as Hugh Low and Company; the Royal Exotic Nursery of Sir Harry Veitch (where the first orchid hybrid, *Calanthe dominyi,* was created in 1856); and the St. Albans nursery of the legendary Frederick Conrad Sander, who, at one point, employed nearly forty orchid collectors. Competition for new species was fierce and it was rumored that collectors would sometimes strip an area to keep the habitat a secret.

These and other independent plant collectors, most of whom received paltry compensation for their efforts under appalling conditions in the field, discovered nearly every orchid species known to science. Many collectors died in the process of searching for new species, and despite persistent reports that the men died from drowning, gunshot and knife wounds, snakebite, trampling by cattle, or blows to the head with blunt instruments, it is generally accepted that in each case the primary cause of death was orchid fever.

Unlike orchid growers today, the big European orchid nurseries of the nineteenth century depended on the massive collection of wild plants. Many of these plants died in transit, but even those that managed to survive and flower didn't last long in cultivation. The growers had little knowledge of healthy growing conditions and did not develop the growing and breeding techniques necessary for the mass production of orchids at more affordable prices. Many of their customers didn't know how to keep the plants alive, disease control was practically nonexistent, and the importance of regulating humidity, heat, light, water, and air circulation was poorly understood. Orchids were also treated as novelty items. They fell in and out of fashion (as they still do today), and all of these factors naturally contributed to high mortality rates and a need to keep re-collecting exotic species of orchids from the wild.

Orchid seeds do not contain endosperm, so they get their nutrients through a complex relationship with microscopic organisms known as mycorrhizal fungi. These fungi invade the dustlike orchid seed and nourish it by converting complex starches into simple sugar. Once the seed has germinated, it turns around and consumes the fungi that helped to give it life. The study of mycorrhizal fungi and their beneficial role in orchid seed germination in the wild was just being discovered in 1909. But this important bit of knowledge, along with the technique of meristem cloning (a technique that produces countless plants that are genetically identical to the parent plant), was not developed in time to help many of the old nurseries make the transition from mass collecting to mass propagation. Outdated marketing strategies also contributed to their decline when the demand for high-priced specimen plants for extravagant private collections eventually died out around the time of World War I. Orchid fever finally subsided in England, and it was not long before institutional and private collections across Europe started to fall into decline. As a fitting symbol of the end of this era, in 1917 the once-magnificent greenhouse of the duke of Devonshire was dynamited because it had become far too expensive to maintain.

To all appearances, orchid fever had burned itself out. In the 1930s many of the formerly grand European orchid firms, especially in England, were still struggling to survive. The importation of huge numbers of orchids had ceased and growers were already acutely aware that artificial propagation was the wave of the future. Decades went by, and with the exception of the cut flower and orchid corsage market following World War II, hardly a ripple of excitement could be detected in the moribund orchid world.

But then, like a peat fire that has smoldered undetected in the subsoil for years, the widespread interest in orchids once again sprang to life. This revival was the direct result of a collaboration by scientists, nurserymen, and plant hunters. They quietly joined forces, and with improved propagation methods, new marketing techniques, and the development of new hybrids, orchid nurseries started to produce and sell large numbers of live plants. The middle class had acquired a passion for house plants, and by the mid-1960s orchid growing was no longer an elitist pastime. The new *Cymbidium, Cattleya,* and *Phalaenopsis* hybrids were inexpensive, thanks to meristem cloning techniques; the blooms were nearly indestructible and long-lasting; and books were available that explained how to grow the things in your backyard or on the kitchen table. Orchids became so cheap and readily available that many people lost interest in growing the same plant year after year. They would simply buy the plants in bloom and then throw them away when the flowers died.

The market had long since shifted from wild-collected exotic species to mass-marketed hybrids produced by huge nurseries worldwide, but by the mid-1980s the orchid world was starting to feel the heat generated by some new players. These people were not growers and they did not buy or collect orchids. They represented powerful botanical institutions and national nursery industries, and it soon became apparent that they were in the business of collecting orchid collectors dealing in rare species, and running them out of business.

This new group consisted primarily of European botanists, lawyers, and informers, and they had determined that large-scale plant collecting, similar to what went on in the mid-nineteenth century, was about to be revived. Fearing that this would lead to the extinction of rare and endangered species of orchids in the wild, they started to strengthen laws that regulated the movement of plants across international borders. They have been called everything from "environmental visionaries" to "ignorant thugs," but in any event these people moved quickly and efficiently and by the end of the 1980s every orchid species and artificial hybrid and all aspects of trade and research had fallen under their control. This seemed like a well-intended and reasonable approach, but unfortunately the trade restrictions immediately increased the desire for the plants, raised their market value dramatically, and led to even more collecting of rare orchid species from the wild.

In the orchid trade, these people are lumped into a group commonly known as the orchid police. The first time I heard the term was in 1996 during an anonymous phone call from a man who said he was a lawyer from Chicago. The man told me he had heard through the grapevine that I had copies of private letters and other documents that could compromise several prominent members of the orchid police. When I told him that I had, indeed, been sent all sorts of curious and shocking information about the professional and private lives of the orchid people, he cautioned me to photocopy the documents and keep the second set in a safe place.

"Orchid police? It sounds terribly sinister, but you are kidding, aren't you?"

"Not at all," he replied. "If these people can raid orchid nurseries, who knows what else they can do? From what I'm told, I don't think it would take much for them to prove you have been in regular contact with some unsavory characters in the orchid world."

The orchid police were beginning to sound fairly unsavory as well. I wanted to talk to them, and so I asked the man on the phone how I might go about finding these people.

"Don't worry," he replied. "If you have the documents I think you have, they will find you."

It was at about this time that I got into the habit of taping my computer disks to the backs of cereal boxes in the kitchen cabinet. Every clicking sound on the phone became a wiretap, bottled-water deliverymen were no longer allowed inside the front door, and e-mail suddenly felt like a very bad way to send confidential messages. There weren't any unexpected service calls from men in unmarked vans asking to inspect the air conditioner that I don't own, but my suspicion of strangers became so acute that eventually I was forced to abandon my habit of talking to Jehovah's Witnesses at the front door, and irrational fear doesn't get much worse than that.

Chapter 5

HENRY AZADEHDEL—
ORCHID COLLECTOR

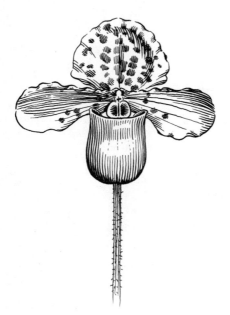

Paphiopedilum henryanum

On a cold day just before Christmas of 1987, a young mother was wheeling her three-month-old child down a quiet suburban sidewalk in the town of Long Eaton, England. As she returned to her house she noticed some men standing on the front porch. When she saw them by the front door, she started to scream.

Thinking the men were robbers, she called out for help from the neighbors, but before anyone could respond to her pleas, the men led the hysterical woman to the house and made her unlock the door. They showed identification, ordered the woman to stay outside with the baby, and then entered the house. It was bitterly cold and both the mother and child were left on the front steps while the men searched the premises.

Sometime later the woman was ordered into the house to make coffee and tea, and while she was complying with this bizarre request the men moved from room to room examining the contents of drawers, looking in closets, and confiscating valuables. These items included a gold necklace, a diamond bracelet, camera equipment, sunglasses, a silver belt buckle, and a CD player. The woman watched in horror as her personal possessions were handled by these men. Before they left the house they removed more than 350 orchids from her husband's greenhouse. The woman was in shock, and she told me later she was consumed by anger and terror. The men didn't close the front door, and after they had finally gone the woman just sat on the floor with her child and wept.

As the woman wandered around her home in a daze, her husband, Henry Azadehdel, was going through his own ordeal. The previous day he had been detained at Heathrow Airport for bringing thirteen *Phragmipedium besseae* orchid seedlings into the United Kingdom without proper CITES permits. The market value of these plants was less than $30 and in those days they were not on the Appendix I endangered list, although, as Appendix II plants, they still required a CITES permit plus a phytosanitary certificate, neither of which Henry had.

Henry Azadehdel was accused of smuggling rare and endangered orchids. He eventually went on trial and the last thing the general public heard about him was that he had pleaded guilty and been convicted on all counts, sentenced to a year in prison, and fined more than $30,000 for plundering rare orchids from jungles around the world. An Associated Press headline read: "Britain Imprisons an Orchid Pirate" and the *Daily Express* ran a story titled "Orchid Smuggler Who Plundered the World." After that, Henry just disappeared.

By the time I started looking for Henry Azadehdel in 1996, no one in the orchid world had heard from him in nearly seven years. When I contacted the nurseries and botanists who had done business with Henry, I received a wide range of responses. Dr. W. W. Wilson of Penn Valley Orchids in Pennsylvania had once nominated Henry for a Gold Award from the American Orchid Society for his discoveries of new orchid species. Another man called him a "son of a bitch" and claimed Henry still owed him $10,000. From what I could gather, Henry Azadehdel was a very controversial and temperamental person. But despite his notorious reputation, no one knew what had become of him. One of the most flamboyant and successful orchid hunters of the late twentieth century had simply vanished.

Then one day in the spring of 1997, I was talking to Norris Powell on the phone. We were discussing the orchid trade when suddenly Norris said, "Hey, I got something for you, baby!"

"What's that, Norris?"

"I just heard from Henry Azadehdel."

"Where is he?"

Norris didn't know, but he had Henry's e-mail address and gave it to me. I sent a message to Henry and then waited. Two weeks went by without a response. Then one morning I checked my messages and there on the screen I saw the words:

WHO ARE YOU?
HENRY

I sent him a message explaining that I wanted to talk to him about his arrest and his work as an orchid collector. His second reply was nearly as brief as the first one. It read:

I HAVE NO NEED TO TALK TO YOU OR ANYONE ELSE ABOUT THESE MATTERS.
HENRY

I waited for a week to go by before contacting him again. I didn't want to scare Henry back into hiding, but I also knew that if I waited too long he would disappear forever. I sent him another message describing how I had read many of the newspaper and magazine accounts of his arrest and that it seemed as if they had all been written from a single source. Henry didn't bother replying to this message.

I had no idea how Henry's story was picked up by the print media, but judging from the quotes, statistics, and overall tone of the articles it seemed to me that a single source had fed the orchid pirate story to the press. In any event, the resulting articles were a stunning tribute to the fine art of British tabloid journalism, and each new account became more shrill and fantastic than the preceding one as the orchid-smuggling story ignited a brief media feeding frenzy. The numbers of smuggled plants at Heathrow quickly increased from 13 to 335, and their value multiplied from £1.30 to £250,000. In a final effort to fill more column space, one writer claimed that Henry smuggled hundreds of wild orchids in order to hang them from the ceiling of his bedroom, because their intoxicating floral scent was a powerful aphrodisiac. With this, the journalistic possibilities were exhausted and the editors went back to the latest round of UFO and Elvis sightings.

Realizing that Henry probably didn't have much regard for writers, I took a chance and sent him a message saying that I had a strong suspicion that some important details had been excluded from the media coverage. I also invited Henry to tell his version of what happened. I didn't expect to hear from him again, and ten days passed before I received this message:

WHAT DO YOU WANT TO KNOW?
HENRY

I have never met Henry Azadehdel and I don't know where he lives. We communicate via e-mail. For the first two years of our correspondence I had no idea what he looked like until I saw a full-page portrait of him in a back issue of the British *Daily Telegraph* weekend magazine. Examining the photograph, I immediately realized that part of Henry's public relations problem was that he looked like an orchid smuggler. Henry was posed facing the camera and he had a penetrating stare of astonishing intensity. He looked threatening and unpredictable. His trim, compact frame suggested intense vitality, and the studio lighting accentuated his sharp, foxlike features, black goatee, and olive complexion, giving him a cruel and satanic look. This look of a demonic orchid thief is exactly what the photographer had in mind, and I have to admit that he captured the image perfectly. The accompanying text was the predictable tale of a rapacious smuggler pillaging rare orchids from the tropical rain forests of the world, and then making a huge profit by selling the plants to wealthy collectors.

I spoke to Henry on the phone once in 1997, and his forceful, clipped manner of speaking had a breathless, conspiratorial tone that fit well with his *Daily Telegraph* photo. I was intrigued to meet him, but after agreeing to an interview at a hotel in London in March 1998, he failed to show up. Shortly after that, I came across a second photo of Henry. This one, from an old issue of the *Independent,* showed Henry clean-shaven, and his long black eyelashes and gentle expression made him look kind, thoughtful, and sensitive. Whoever he might be, it was clear to me that Henry Azadehdel was a very complex character.

Henry is Armenian by birth. In addition to his work with orchids he was once employed as a diplomatic aide in Tehran during the time of the shah. Henry is often portrayed as being paranoid, devious, and untrustworthy; but this not a balanced assessment, because his character has a public-spirited and charitable side. In 1991, as part of the British Gulf Aid project, Henry was instrumental in gathering and organizing the delivery of hundreds of tons of food, two field hospitals, blankets, medicine, tents, winter clothing, baby food, and other emergency supplies to Kurdish refugee camps along the Iran-Iraq border. Despite all the terrible things that had been said about him in the popular press, I found the contradictions in Henry's appearance and behavior immensely appealing.

The pieces of the Henry Azadehdel puzzle are numerous and well scattered and I never expect to understand fully what sort of man he is. Henry is an enigma and I am confident that he will always remain mysterious and unknowable. Letters of support and photocopied business correspondence from his network of botanical institutions and commercial orchid growers still arrive from places like Sumatra, the Isle of Jersey, Moscow, Australia, Java, the Philippines, California, Yunnan, India, Frankfurt, and other parts of the world. The information contained in these and other documents has given me a small window into Henry's world, but even then it has taken me years to understand the extent of his orchid collecting and details of his downfall.

At first, Henry would only provide me with vague hints about his work collecting orchids. For example, he might give me the name of an orchid, a date, a CITES permit number, and the name of a botanical institution to see if I could make the connections. There was a two-week period in my life when each morning I would get up to read yet another e-mail orchid clue from Henry Azadehdel. It was a game to test my intuition and to see how much I knew about the orchid world. I have to admit I knew very little at that point, but it was enough to keep Henry's interest. During this time he made discreet inquiries about me, and within two months of his first message he was explaining the details of his orchid collecting in the mid-1980s. According to Henry, his clients included some of the most prominent botanical institutions in the world.

Tropical orchid hunting can be a dangerous and unpleasant business, and it usually involves long journeys into remote jungle areas that are cut off from the outside world. Traveling and working in tropical forests is never easy and plant collectors often face formidable challenges, some of them life-threatening.

For example, the beautiful and highly sought-after *Paphiopedilum delenatii* is found in parts of Vietnam. Unfortunately, several of the prime habitats are still dotted with land mines. This is enough to discourage most orchid hunters, but Henry has been to these areas several times, and they provide him with the sort of excitement that he craves. In the first half of the 1980s Henry discovered dozens of pristine orchid sites in southern China, especially Guizhou, Guangxi, and Yunnan provinces, all of which contain prime habitat for *Paphiopedilum malipoense,* a stunning slipper orchid with lime-green petals marked with purple veining and a large waxy pouch that emits a delicious, raspberry-scented fragrance. In addition to the remote corners of Vietnam and China, Henry has traveled extensively throughout Hainan Island, Papua New Guinea, Irian Jaya, the Solomon Islands, Borneo, North Sumatra, Thailand, and, no doubt, many other places that he will never tell me about.

Orchid-collecting expeditions are expensive and time-consuming affairs, and there is no guarantee of success. Only a handful of skilled collectors, like Henry, working in conjunction with local villagers, know where to look for the best examples of new or exotic orchid species. These collectors are in the business of finding and selling limited quantities of select breeding plants. They tend to travel on their own and, with very few exceptions, they don't talk about the details of their work with strangers. In the orchid world, only a very small number of collectors possess the botanical knowledge, physical stamina, and dedication to search for rare species in the wild.

The most common type of orchid hunter doesn't sell plants. These are people like Donald and Richard, the two men I took to Fire Mountain. They journey to remote areas at their own expense and undergo the same appalling travel conditions as the professional collectors; and while they may collect a plant or two for themselves or a leaf tip for laboratory analysis, their primary goal is to study how the orchids grow in their native habitat. One of the many popular myths about orchid collecting describes how rare plants are being thoughtlessly ripped from the jungle by the tens or hundreds of thousands, jammed into boxes, and later sold, half-dead, for a quick, easy profit. Having watched the process many times, I can assure you that the delicate and time-consuming operation is carried out with the surgical precision of an organ transplant.

Any botanical institution or commercial nursery that is conducting significant work with orchids or other rare plants has a network of "unofficial" collectors. It is the only reasonable and affordable way to get access to the plant material. The unofficial collectors, like Henry, also know how to illegally transport plants across international borders, and anyone who thinks that the CITES permit system for orchids is applied equally to commercial growers and well-connected botanical institutions is badly misinformed. According to orchid-world insiders, the primary difference between an orchid collector and an orchid smuggler is this: an orchid collector works for a prestigious botanical institution, while an orchid smuggler works for a commercial orchid nursery. The species of plants and the habitats where they are collected are the same.

While Henry and I were slowly getting to know each other I decided to talk to Dr. Harold Koopowitz, author of the popular book *Plant Extinction—A Global Crisis.* Harold is a world authority on the feeding behavior of the polyclad flatworm, *Planocera gilchristi,* but he is far better known for his extensive knowledge about the orchid trade and his opinions on plant conservation. Along with Norito Hasegawa, he is co-owner of the orchid nursery Paphanatics in southern California. He is also a highly respected professor of ecology and conservation biology at the University of California at Irvine. Harold was brought up in South Africa and he has a special interest in the orchids of Zimbabwe, where he is studying population ecology by taking leaf samples and analyzing the DNA.

Generally speaking, there are two types of orchid researchers. The first type likes to go out into the wild to study plants in their natural habitat. The second type prefers to collect the plants, bring them back to the lab, and pulverize them in a blender to study the DNA. Fortunately, Harold's research combines both of these approaches and for this reason his work on orchids is highly regarded by scientists and commercial growers. "In laymen's terms, I'm looking for the mommy plants and the daddy plants in order to understand the distribution dynamics," Harold says.

At a meeting with Harold in Santa Barbara, California, he pointed out that Henry Azadehdel wasn't bringing in excessively large quantities of orchids. He was collecting small numbers of very choice plants for both commercial growers and botanists. Some were sold and others were donated. These plants were relatively rare in cultivation and very little was known about their status in the wild. Harold went on to explain that CITES officials were very quick to say these plants came from endangered populations, in order to "err on the safe side."

"It was only after Henry's arrest that things started to heat up," Harold explained. Harold felt that the extreme media coverage surrounding Henry's arrest helped to push through CITES regulations to move all slipper orchids, both paphiopedilums and their South American cousins the phragmipediums, onto the Appendix I endangered list. "This resolution," Harold continued, "had a profound effect on the orchid world because it changed Appendix I from dealing with truly rare plants to abolishing all trade in a large group of orchids on the off chance that some of them might be rare. Not a good idea, and you can imagine the uproar that this caused with scientists and growers."

I have studied the Dutch proposal closely, and only recently did I discover that it had been presented at the CITES meeting in Lausanne in 1989 by Ger van Vliet, who at the time was working at the Leiden Botanic Garden. Comments on the endangered status of each *Paphiopedilum* species was based almost solely on habitat and trade information supplied by Phillip Cribb at Kew and Ger van Vliet, who now admits some of the data was incomplete. According to Dr. van Vliet, due to budget restraints the German *Phragmipedium* proposal was presented by a Dr. Jelden who specializes in reptiles.

When I asked Harold for his thoughts on CITES trade restrictions on orchids, he replied: "Well, considering how only 0.01 percent of plant extinction is trade-related, it is a mystery how these people became so powerful. One of the good things about CITES is that it has drawn attention to the plight of plants. Before CITES, all attention was on elephants and the cute furry animals of the world. This attempt to control the trade in endangered plants is a very good idea, but only as part of a more comprehensive plan that also includes habitat protection and artificial propagation. I guess the nicest thing I can say about the organization, as it applies to orchids, is that it is autocratic and dictatorial with no due process or court of appeal. It is run by a handful of people who are trying to regulate a diverse field of study and a huge industry of which they have little knowledge."

Harold went on to tell me about a series of television programs about plant conservation that came out about a year after Henry was arrested at Heathrow Airport. "In one of the episodes," Harold said, "a plant officer from IUCN [World Conservation Union] held up a specimen of *Paphiopedilum bellatulum* as an example of one of these highly and critically endangered orchids. Not terribly convincing. It may be difficult to cultivate in a nursery, but the thing grows like a weed in the wild and is widespread. The man might as well have been holding a cabbage for all that he impressed the scientific community with his knowledge of orchid conservation."

Harold believes that with today's modern propagation techniques, there was no need to import large numbers of orchids or to halt all trade. If it was legal to import limited numbers of wild-collected Appendix I orchid seed pods and orchids for breeding, the commercial nursery business could easily mass-produce a worldwide supply of these plants. Based on his eight-year study of the South African orchid *Aerangis verdickii*, Harold and his graduate students have discovered that, on average, one out of one million of these orchid seeds will grow into a mature plant in the wild. With such a paltry reproduction rate, there is no scientific or logical basis to prohibit the trade in orchid seeds. In addition to this finding, some serious botanists and most orchid breeders insist that trade laws that prohibit the importation of Appendix I and other orchid seeds hinder ex situ conservation because new seeds are essential to strengthening the gene pool and increasing plant resistance to disease.

"And getting back to Henry," Harold said, "Whether you love or hate the man, there is no denying the fact that he was a very talented collector. He did a lot of good and *Paphiopedilum henryanum* was named after him for his contribution to orchid science and conservation."

Henry has a flair for the dramatic and he takes a perverse pleasure in slowly revealing facts. After months of promising to do so, he started feeding me a steady stream of old personal correspondence and other documents. Up until this time, I had only read the outrageous tabloid accounts of Henry Azadehdel, the orchid pirate. But as I began to look through this new material, it dawned on me that Henry's story was far more complicated than the superficial accounts that appeared in the media. For the first time, I could see tangible proof that Henry had been significantly involved with many of the leading botanists in the orchid world. According to several letters, dating from the mid-1980s, Henry had shared his orchid discoveries with people like Alexander Vasiljev at the Main Botanical Gardens in Moscow; Dr. Gustav Schoser, director of the Palmengarten in Frankfurt; and another great orchid hunter, the late Dr. Jack Fowlie, who was the editor of *Orchid Digest* magazine in California.

The most intriguing letters, also dating from the mid-1980s, came from botanists at the Royal Botanic Gardens, Kew. The letters, all written on Kew stationery, detailed the receipt of rare orchids from Henry. One botanist thanked him for providing seed for the micropropagation unit at Kew, while others made requests for desirable species of rare orchids. To further substantiate these transactions, Henry Azadehdel provided me with copies of invoices and letters from orchid nurseries in Asia that, on Henry's instructions, had shipped rare and protected tropical orchids to Kew from 1984 to 1986. The nurseries included Shahnas Orchids in Sumatra, C. L. Bundt in Sulawesi, and Diamond Farm in Kowloon. One invoice listed numbers of plants, species, and prices.

Henry also sent me copies of his U.K. CITES import permits for rare orchids that had been arranged for him by Kew. Two of his permits—U.K. CITES permit #P3698, issued December 19, 1984, for *Paphiopedilum micranthum*; and U.K. CITES permit #P3757, issued February 15, 1985, for *P. devogelii* (an undescribed species, later identified as *P. supardii*). Both permits were filled out incorrectly and incompletely, which allowed for the import of wild-collected, CITES-protected plants. CITES permits for rare plants, especially orchids, are not issued without very close scrutiny, and it is important to point out that the CITES officer in charge of issuing U.K. import permits and examining the plants has his office at Kew and is on the advisory board of the Kew Herbarium. Henry claims that these two permits show how a preferential permit system allowed him to bring these plants into the United Kingdom despite the CITES regulations.

The raid on Henry Azadehdel's home was carried out by H.M.S. Customs and Excise, with the assistance of Dr. Phillip Cribb, a botanist from the Royal Botanic Gardens, Kew. According to customs officials, Dr. Cribb was there as a professional expert to assist in identifying plants.

When I later asked the press officer at H.M.S. Customs and Excise what sort of warrant was issued for the raid, I was told that no warrant was necessary because the Azadehdel home was searched under the Police and Criminal Evidence Act, section 18, subsection 1. This, according to the officer, is a provision that allows for a search of the premises of any person who is under arrest. The search, I was informed, was for evidence relating to the offense for which Henry had been arrested. This didn't sound quite right to me, because if the purpose of the operation was to confiscate illegal orchids kept in a backyard greenhouse, what were the customs officers doing rummaging around in the bedrooms and other parts of the house? And if they were looking for orchids, what was the rationale behind the confiscation of camera equipment, jewelry, and other valuables? When I asked the press officer about the confiscation of personal items, she told me that those items were taken because they were goods that were under suspicion of having been smuggled into this country without paying the correct customs duty. "If officers happen across other items relating to other crimes when seeking evidence for a particular offense [in this case, orchid smuggling], they may seize those items as well," she explained.

After the raid on Henry's home, the orchids from his greenhouse were taken from Long Eaton to the Royal Botanic Gardens, Kew. Very shortly thereafter, and long before court-appointed experts could examine and identify the plants, the orchids were repotted and the plant name tags were removed. In addition to this, root tips were broken off and trimmed, which destroyed evidence of how long the orchids had been in cultivation. This would make it virtually impossible to determine whether the plants had been nursery-grown or collected from the wild, as the prosecution would later claim. Few of the orchids were in bloom at the time of the raid, and without the original plant labels, identification was very difficult to determine.

This repotting of the evidence wasn't the only problem. The orchids had been taken to Kew for "safekeeping," but by the time Dr. Pamela Burns-Balogh, an orchidology expert for the defense, was given a brief opportunity to examine the confiscated plants, many of them had already died and the rest were in very poor condition. They were infested with scale, mealybugs, and ants, and recently laid insect eggs were visible on the lower leaves. In addition to this, she observed broken, split, and blistered leaves, water and insecticide damage, and fungal and viral infections. Any one of these, she pointed out in her detailed report, "may cause irreparable damage and death to the plants." She urged the court to move the plants to a neutral facility where they could be taken care of properly, but her request was denied.

According to court documents, of the 365 confiscated plants, 44 were nursery-grown hybrids and therefore perfectly legal. Of the remaining plants, 139 had either proper CITES permits or receipts from local British nurseries. Many of the other plants were either gifts or divisions of orchids that Henry had originally collected for Kew. Unfortunately, these details were never reported in the local press. According to the tabloid accounts, all 365 plants were wild-collected species of endangered orchids that had been stripped from the jungle by Henry Azadehdel, the orchid pirate. This is a myth that endures to the present day.

None of Henry Azadehdel's orchids has ever been returned to him. Curious about the fate of these plants, in August 1999 I contacted Sandra Bell, who is in charge of the live orchid collection at Kew Gardens. I sent her a courteous e-mail message asking if she could help me determine how many of Henry's orchids were still alive. I also wanted to know if she could describe the condition of the plants and let me know how they were being used. In response, I received a rather frosty reply stating that it was not the policy of Kew to respond to queries regarding confiscated plant material.

It was for thirteen illegally imported CITES Appendix II orchids worth approximately $30 that Henry Azadehdel had his home raided by British customs officials and £42,000 worth of orchids confiscated. In addition to this, he spent five weeks in jail and his wife had to undergo psychiatric treatment for trauma caused by the raid on her home.

Eighteen months after his arrest for smuggling orchids, the

charges against Henry Azadehdel were reduced on appeal. He was fined a total of £2,500, and his prison sentence was limited to the five weeks already served. During Henry's stay in jail his fellow prisoners wondered why he was doing time for flowers while his wife and two young children were left to fend for themselves. Most of these men were in prison for violent crimes— armed robbery, housebreaking, assault and battery, and the like. After ten years, Henry can laugh about what happened to him. He has told me that he can forgive his tormentors for what they did to him, but not for the pain they caused his family.

Henry Azadehdel has openly admitted to collecting, donating, and selling wild orchids. He is proud of his discoveries of new orchid species and his contribution to scientific research, but to this day Henry remains a mystery man. We continue our correspondence, but he is far too elusive and complex a character to understand. For all I know he may be slippery, shrewd, unpredictable, and calculating, as his critics contend, but based on the facts of his case and how the authorities treated him, it is clear that his ordeal had very little to do with orchid conservation, the protection of rare plants, or a fair and reasonable legal procedure.

The idea of course, had been to make a highly publicized example of Henry. He was investigated and prosecuted in an effort to caution other orchid collectors and to help raise public awareness about the trade in endangered plant species. I don't know if Henry is still collecting orchids. I assume he is, but what I find most curious about these events is that after all the time, expense, and effort to vilify Henry Azadehdel, now the authorities don't want to talk about him.

Chapter 6

THE FOX TESTICLE
ICE CREAM OF KEMAL
KUCUKONDERUZUNKOLUK

Orchis provincialis

I was exhausted from the effort of trying to keep up with the complex battles that were being fought on the British horticultural scene. Following my convoluted discussions with Henry Azadehdel, I felt as if I had been caught up in the rarefied world of plant politics and distracted from my focus on orchids. I needed something fresh and uplifting to rekindle my interest in the plants, so I called my friend Eleanor Kerrigan in Seattle to ask her if she had any new or unusual orchid stories for me.

"Orchid ice cream," she said. "Made from what the Renaissance nurserymen called 'bollock grass.' Check it out."

Eleanor directed me to *Orchid Biology*, a fine collection of scientific articles written by some of the most distinguished and obscure orchidologists on earth. In Volume 3 of the series I discovered that Leonard J. Lawler, in his piece "The Ethnobotany of the Orchidaceae," had quite a lot of interesting things to say about bollock grass, which included a few historical references to orchid ice cream. Lawler is well known for his intrepid scholarship, especially in the field of orchid esoterica, and it was with his help that I eventually stumbled upon a strange tale of a Turkish dessert made from wild orchid tubers, milk, and sugar. The frozen mixture was beaten with metal rods, eaten with a knife and fork, and so elastic that it could be stretched into a jump rope.

Orchid ice cream jump rope? This is the sort of material that can keep me awake at night. On a whim I called the editorial office of *Natural History* magazine in New York suggesting that I write a story for them about the orchid ice cream of Turkey. At first they thought the story proposal was a joke, but I persisted with the idea until they finally relented and gave me an assignment to investigate the rumors. A month later I was standing at the railing of an aging ferryboat as it crossed the Bosporus, headed for the Asian shore of Istanbul.

With the Galata Bridge and the domed silhouette of Hagia Sophia receding in our wake, I contemplated a dessert that, according to the experts, could heal the spleen, prevent cholera and tuberculosis, facilitate childbirth, stop your hands and feet from shaking, and improve your sex life. A crudely translated book on Turkish herbal medicine (which I found in Sahaflar Carsisi—the old book bazaar located just off Cadircilar Caddesi) explained how wild orchid tuber ice cream "will cure those who mentally fallen crazy in love." These product claims seemed doubtful, even by Western marketing standards, so to investigate the tantalizing rumors, I was on my way to visit Ali Kumbasar, a man who had been making orchid ice cream in Istanbul for more than twenty-eight years.

Ali and his four brothers run Ali Usta, an ice cream shop in the fashionable neighborhood of Moda, and it was there that I took my first bite of *salepi dondurma,* the orchid ice cream of Turkey. At Ali Usta there are thirty-two flavors, but I was primarily interested in the original, plain flavor. It looked like vanilla ice cream and came with a variety of toppings that included freshly ground pistachio nuts, dark curls of shaved chocolate, and bits of toasted almond. It was creamy like gelato, but surprisingly chewy, with a smoothness and texture that was entirely new to me. It was also delicious.

Ali explained that *dondurma* is the Turkish word for ice cream, and that the essential ingredient of orchid ice cream is *salep,* a whitish flour milled from the dried tubers of certain wild, terrestrial orchids. Similar orchids grow throughout Europe, the eastern Mediterranean, and Asia Minor, but the orchid tubers used for this uniquely Turkish delicacy come from the mountainous edges of the Anatolian plateau. Species of the genus *Orchis* (mainly O. *latifolia,* O. *mascula,* O. *maculata,* and O. *anatolica*) are said to be the best sources of orchid flour, and villagers collect the paired tubers of each plant during the spring and summer months.

Salep dealers say that the most valuable tubers for ice cream are the ones that dry to the translucent yellow color of alabaster. This translucence indicates a more complex flavor and a higher percentage of mucilage, a gluelike substance similar to cellulose that often makes up nearly 45 percent of *salep*. The mucilage gives orchid ice cream its distinctive firmness, and makes it necessary to use a knife and fork when eating it, even during the summer. In the living plant, mucilage helps the tubers retain water and lowers the freezing point of the plant tissue, making the orchids less susceptible to drought and frost. To be honest, this bit about the mucilage didn't interest me all that much, but I figured I should throw it into the story because it was just the sort of information that the editors at *Natural History* magazine would relish.

The word *salep* comes from the Arabic *sahlab,* which means "testicles of the fox." Ali showed me a handful of the dried tubers, and although I have never had the opportunity to examine a fox that closely, the paired, ovoid spheres did bear a striking resemblance to that part of the human male anatomy.

Ancient accounts referred to this similarity, and the first-century A.D. Greek physician Dioscorides recommended the use of orchid tubers as an aphrodisiac. Linnaeus, writing in 1751, also mentioned the use of *salep* as an aphrodisiac. The word *orchis* in Greek means "testicle," so it seems that European interest in orchids was originally focused on the erotic aftereffects of eating the tubers rather than on the appreciation of beautiful flowers.

"Fox testicle ice cream"—the literal translation of *salepi dondurma*—didn't seem like an appropriate name for the glass dessert dish filled with colorful scoops of ice cream that Ali placed on the table in front of me. The cold, silky orbs held the familiar flavors of apricot, pistachio, red currant, peach, vanilla, and bilberry, but there was a subtle aftertaste that I couldn't identify—slightly sweet with a subtle, nutty flavor similar to dried milk powder. It also had a hint of mushrooms, yak butter, and the smell of a goat on a rainy day. Not unpleasant, but an earthy, lanolin fragrance that added an intriguing dimension to the ice cream as it slowly melted in my mouth.

Ali told me that *salepi dondurma* was first made in eastern Anatolia in the sixteenth century. I don't know from where he obtained this bit of information, but I later came across a European account of Turkish fruit sorbets in *Les Observations de Plusieurs Singularités et Choses Mémorables*. Published in 1553 and written by Pierre Belon, a French botanist who traveled through Turkey and Asia Minor, this book confirms that iced desserts were common in Turkey at that time.

Western food scholars continue to debate the precise dates, locations, and origins of frozen desserts, but most Turkish ice cream enthusiasts have long since agreed that *salepi dondurma* originally came from Maras, a city located in south-central Turkey on the eastern slopes of the Taurus Mountains. Several species of orchids grow nearby, milk is available from cattle, sheep, and goats, and snow is abundant for the freezing process. Similar orchid habitats exist elsewhere in Turkey, especially near Mount Ararat and Lake Van to the east, but for the Turkish people Maras is the home of orchid ice cream.

A hot drink, also called *salep,* is made from dried orchid tuber flour, sugar, milk, and cinnamon. For hundreds of years it has been served during the cold winter months in Greece, Turkey, Syria, and even England, where it was called "saloop." Today, when Turkish men claim that the beverage is used for strengthening the body, it is abundantly clear which part of the body they are referring to.

Ali speculated that the first batch of *salepi dondurma* was probably a mistake—the result of a pot of hot *salep* freezing overnight. In an attempt to save his valuable ingredients, the *salep* vendor probably chipped and pried at the frozen mixture with a metal rod in an attempt to extract it from the pot. The stiffened mass of milk, sugar, and *salep* turned out to be rather tasty, and this discovery led to further refinements. In time, the *salep* vendors developed the technique of kneading the mass of *dondurma* to a smooth consistency using hand-forged metal rods, similar to the *dondurma* rods manufactured by Turkish blacksmiths today. Ali advised me to go to Maras if I wanted to learn more about traditional *salepi dondurma*. There, I could meet the master ice cream beaters and follow the entire operation, from the collecting of orchid tubers to the finished product.

The modern city of Maras, with its rapidly growing population of more than 350,000 people, is nestled at the edge of the Taurus Mountains. From the air, the surrounding landscape is a patchwork of green fields and rust-red squares of freshly plowed earth extending to undulating slopes and snow-capped peaks in the distance. Pistachio trees dot the fields. As the plane made its final approach to the runway, I could see large flocks of sheep on the hillsides and the tents of nomadic shepherds.

I drove into Maras by cab, and within minutes of my arrival I met Mevlut Dogan, an impeccably dressed sidewalk sage with a four-foot-wide handlebar mustache, the tips of which he had fastened to the shoulders of his suit jacket with brass safety pins. Mevlut described himself as "just an ordinary citizen," and he took me to my first orchid ice cream shop in Maras.

At Yasar Pastenesi, the most elegant *dondurma* shop in town, I watched a man attack the inside of a frozen metal container with a four-foot-long stainless steel rod. He jabbed and twisted his tool, throwing his entire weight into his work, as schoolgirls, young couples, and elderly villagers quietly lined up in front of the shop. From a distance, it appeared as if he was attempting to pry linoleum or tar from the bottom of the container with a large crowbar, but he was merely scooping out portions of ice cream. He reached into the container with his bare hand and produced a white lump that he shoved onto a cone, dipped into a bowl of ground pistachios, and handed it to the next customer in line. When our turn came, Mevlut reminded me, "If you eat *dondurma,* your sex life get stronger. It also prevent you getting lump on your back, and keep your chest soft . . . and heal bronchitis, too."

After we ate our *dondurma,* Mevlut introduced me to the store's owner, Mohammed Kambur, a fourth-generation ice cream maker and the city's largest producer of *salepi dondurma.* Mohammed told me that orchid ice cream had been made in Maras for more than three hundred years. His great-grandfather had brought snow and ice down from the mountains to use in freezing the *dondurma.* To show me how far the business had come since the days of hauling donkey-loads of ice down from the winter snow fields, Mohammed took me on a tour of his modern ice cream factory, with its stainless-steel machinery and crisply uniformed workers. *Salepi dondurma* was originally mixed by hand, using tubs of salted ice water to freeze the mixture. It was then pounded to a smooth consistency with metal rods, and then stretched by hand. Today, Mohammed uses gelato machines imported from Italy. They accomplish the task of freezing the proper proportions of milk, sugar, and *salep* flour, but the final product is still beaten and kneaded with metal rods for at least twenty minutes to achieve the proper degree of elasticity. The recipe for the taffylike *dondurma* has changed slightly, but it is still customary to eat it with a knife and fork.

In Mohammed's office, I followed the glassy-eyed stare of a stuffed mallard perched on top of a bookcase. The bird faced a wall where I examined a framed photograph of a young boy jumping rope. Mohammed wasted no time pointing out that the thick white rope was a length of orchid ice cream. Clearly, this was a dessert to be reckoned with. Obviously the orchid ice cream jump rope rumors were true, so what about the medical benefits and the use of orchid tubers as an aphrodisiac?

For the next two days Mohammed and I drove into the mountains looking for orchids in bloom. It was early spring and as we traveled through swamp meadows and grasslands we found large populations of orchids, but none in flower. We continued our drive along precipitous mountain tracks until we finally began to see plants putting up their flowering spikes. We left the vehicle and climbed through a scattered pine forest and across rocky slopes. Far below us I could make out the distant mountain villages. I heard animal bells farther up the slope, and women's voices, but we saw no one and the voices fell silent as we approached. At the base of a pine tree, growing in a deep mat of pine needles, we came upon our first blooming orchid. Six white flowers were clustered at the top of the loose flower spike. Farther along, the plants became quite numerous, the flowers distinguished by long, thin, upward-pointing spurs. I couldn't make a positive identification at the time, but I took a photograph of the plant and later matched it with a dried herbarium specimen of *Orchis provincialis* at the Royal Botanic Gardens, Kew.

Mohammed dug up the plant to show me the twin tubers. One, slightly discolored and withered, was from the previous year. The other tuber was fresh and white; this is the one that is collected. The villagers wash the fresh tubers and then immerse them in hot water for about fifteen minutes. This is to soften them and to help loosen the outer skin. The tubers are then threaded onto strings and dried in the sun for about a week. Mohammed calculated that two pounds of fresh orchid tubers weigh about ten ounces when dry.

All *salep* used for making ice cream comes from wild-collected plants. Local people claim the orchids are abundant and that this is why no one has made a serious attempt to propagate them artificially in nurseries. Mohammed's level of production requires approximately two and a half tons of dried orchid tubers each year. He has no problem obtaining this quantity locally, and when I asked what effect his ice cream business had on the wild orchid population, he explained that the mountains were still covered with the plants. According to Mohammed, the collecting areas, and the species used, change from year to year, depending on rainfall; and normal fluctuating weather patterns prevent any one habitat from being overcollected.

Others in Turkey are concerned about the overcollection of orchid species, and this has encouraged researchers at Ankara University to start looking into the possibility of growing terrestrial orchids as a farm crop. A longer-term project involves the search for a suitable chemical substitute for *salep*. So far, no one has taken the obvious first step of conducting a population survey to determine what, if any, effect ice cream production in Turkey has had on the wild orchid population.

Back in Maras, Mohammed introduced me to Mehmet Adnan Dedeoglu, who runs a wholesale business in dried *salep,* morel mushrooms, beeswax, lemon-scented cologne, cooking oil, and fox skins. Mehmet brought out strands of dried *salep* for me to look at. He depends on villagers and nomadic shepherds to bring him the *salep,* which he grades and then sells either loose, on the strings, or in powdered form. Most people prefer to buy *salep* as dried tubers, because some dealers cut the *salep* flour with inferior ingredients. The best quality is known as *salepi Maras.* It comes from the mountains and sells for approximately 5 million Turkish lira per kilo. This works out to about $66 per pound. I wanted to try making *salepi dondurma* in my hand-cranked ice cream machine, so before leaving Mehmet's shop I bought a one-kilo bag of the white powder to take home with me.

We also called on Kemal Kucukonderuzunkoluk (pronounced *Kucukonderuzunkoluk*), who operates one of the oldest ice cream stores in Maras. After fifty years of beating *salepi dondurma* with an iron rod, Kemal was still enthusiastic about his ice cream. Like most *dondurma* shops in Maras, Kemal's is a modest operation, and he makes the ice cream by hand in small batches. When he learned that I had traveled from the United States to visit his shop he insisted that I try orchid ice cream every way he could prepare it. At a two-hour tasting session we ate *dondurma* with baklava, *dondurma* with chocolate, *dondurma* with crushed, roasted hazelnuts, *dondurma* sprinkled with ground pistachios, and *dondurma* with fresh strawberries. The *dondurma* arrived on plates, in dessert dishes, and on chocolate-dipped cones, but thankfully, not in the form of a jump rope, because leaping off the ground was clearly out of the question. As I lurched toward the door, a final morsel of ice cream was offered to me from the tip of the stainless-steel *dondurma* stick.

As I lay on my bed at the hotel that afternoon, it was too early to evaluate the long-term health benefits that may result from eating this quantity of orchid ice cream, but the short-term prognosis was excellent. No signs of cholera or tuberculosis, no lump on the back, and no problems with the spleen. As for orchid ice cream's effect on one's sex life, opinions vary. It seems to affect people in different ways, but if the long lines of men waiting for their ice cream cones in Maras are any indication, we can live in hope.

From Maras I flew back to Istanbul and then to New York, where I stood in line to clear U.S. customs. Suddenly I remembered the clear plastic bag of white *salep* powder that I had bought in Maras. Just as I realized that it looked exactly like a one-kilogram bag of heroin, I was motioned to the inspection counter. The officer rummaged through my suitcase and lifted out the bag of white powder.

"Well, what do we have here?" he asked.

"Dried orchid tuber powder for making fox testicle ice cream," I explained.

"Fox . . . testicle . . . ice cream?"

"A Turkish delicacy."

The officer digested this information for a few moments. He looked at me, looked at the bag, and then with a barely audible grunt of disgust, he tossed the packet of white powder back into the suitcase and waved me through.

Chapter 7

AU YONG AND
THE POLLEN THIEF

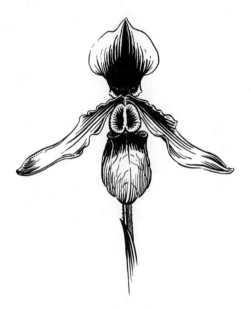

Paphiopedilum hookerae

"You must discover yourself through daily life," said sixty-three-year-old Au Yong Nang Yip as he drove his clenched fist into a pail of sand. I could feel the concrete floor vibrate beneath my feet with each impact. He was building calluses on his knuckles while we talked about orchids.

Au Yong has spent his entire life in Sarawak, the East Malaysian state on the northern coast of Borneo. He explained how, as a young man growing up in Kuching, a town on the South China Sea, he had gone through a bad period of his life. His older brother had forced him out of the family clothing business and Au Yong found himself without an income to support his wife and children. Au Yong's moods became unpredictable and his temper started to take control of his life.

"I had this anger growing in me," he explained. "It burned like a hot coal in my head."

On three occasions he was stopped on the street by a different stranger, and each time the stranger delivered the same message: "Look at your face in the mirror. You are going to kill someone."

Very funny, Au Yong thought to himself. He managed to ignore these warnings until the day he went to visit a local *bomo* (sorcerer) for advice and guidance. The old man confirmed that Au Yong was a natural-born killer. The signs were clearly conveyed by his posture and demeanor. The *bomo* made Au Yong wear a *jeemat* (magic charm) to help him control the anger, but he also told him that he must embrace religion before it was too late. Otherwise he would kill a man within the year. Au Yong wore the yellow, black, and red cloth charm on a string around his neck from 1962 until 1968, but instead of religion, he turned his interest to orchid growing and found his salvation in the mysteries of these plants. In 1969, the year Au Yong opened his orchid business, the charm mysteriously disappeared one night.

Au Yong is a stout and powerfully built man. He has a penetrating stare that is unnerving to strangers, and his face can express terrible cruelty one moment and then exude a Zenlike calm the next. Sitting perfectly still, he radiates an intense vitality. Only a fool would take him lightly. Local people treat him with respect and fear because they are convinced that he has supernatural powers, which may be true. Years ago, when I was first getting to know Au Yong, a man walked up to us to ask a question in Cantonese. Instead of answering the question, Au Yong glared at the man for about thirty seconds until the man fainted. I have never fully understood what happened that day. We never discussed the incident, but I have always assumed that this is only one example of the sort of power that he can exert over people.

Au Yong is also an honorable man who leads a simple existence, free of all pretense. He lives with his extended family in a traditional Chinese home that is surrounded by his orchid nursery, which is called Orchidwoods. The view from the windows in the house is dominated by a sea of colorful orchids that extends to the property line in every direction. In addition to his nursery, he owns an Esso service station and runs a video and television repair shop. He left school after the fifth grade, but through hard work, persistence, and a fierce devotion to his family, he managed to send several of his children to university in the United States. One of his sons is a doctor in New York City.

To the Western mind, Au Yong is a complex man full of contradictions. But these same contradictions in the Asian context are considered to be essential for creating balance in a person's character. For example, he describes himself as a devout Buddhist, yet he openly practices black magic and is an active member of the Christian community. He is an accomplished traditional Chinese herbalist, but he also prepares special potions on the full moon to bring good luck, love, or good health. On any given day people come to Au Yong for small vials of these useful concoctions.

Despite his obvious success in a wide variety of business ventures, Au Yong dresses casually in baggy shorts, rubber thongs, and a clean white sleeveless undershirt that shows off his broad shoulders and smooth, massive arms. He is a master of T'ai Chi, but he also devotes part of each day to lifting weights and pounding his fists and feet against a wooden post for martial arts training. The rest of his time is spent caring for his orchids. This odd combination of extreme violence and aestheticism is part of what makes Au Yong such an irresistible and unique character.

Orchidwoods supplies the local cut flower market with colorful sprays of dendrobium hybrids, but Au Yong's international reputation was built on his knowledge of the native orchid species of Borneo. In 1975 he was the one who reintroduced *Paphiopedilum hookerae* into cultivation with the help and collaboration of his friend Fumi Sugiami, a highly respected Japanese orchid grower. Au Yong's nursery list reads like a roll call of Borneo's greatest orchid hits. There are the paphiopedilums— *stoneii, amabile, sanderianum, volonteanum, rothschildianum,* and *lowii*—as well as spectacular examples of *Phalaenopsis violacea* (especially the white alba form) and assorted *Bulbophyllum* species.

One of the most unusual orchids in Au Yong's collection is *Bulbophyllum beccarii,* which is named after the Italian botanist Odoardo Beccari, who visited Sarawak around the turn of the century. Beccari described the plant as smelling like a thousand dead elephants. This stink of carrion attracts clouds of flies, which are the orchid's pollinating insects. *Bulbophyllum beccarii* is also notoriously difficult to grow. It takes up a tremendous amount of space in a greenhouse. The flowers are ugly, small, and insignificant, so naturally there are orchid people who can't resist trying to grow the thing.

Every year orchid growers from around the world come to pay homage to Au Yong, who makes the modest claim that his interest in orchids is just a hobby. Clearly, his business is far more than a pastime, and anyone who is serious about Borneo orchids sooner or later comes to Au Yong's house on Rock Road in Kuching to meet with the master.

The stream of visitors also includes academics, botanists, photographers, plant historians, orchid hunters, authors, and anyone else who is even remotely interested in Borneo orchids. He offers a warm yet gruff hospitality, but he is also the sort of person who has no patience for opportunists or fools; for this reason not everyone who drops by for a visit remembers the encounter with fondness.

"I used to take people into the jungle to look at orchids, but no more," Au Yong told me. "Dr. Jack Fowlie, Earl Ross, Dr. Asher, Tony Lamb, and Phillip Cribb from Kew. All famous people now. They all come to me for information. I take them to look at *Paphiopedilum stoneii,* and *Bulbophyllum,* and every orchid they want. I drive my own car and in the jungle I carry everything—food, water, equipment. I work like hell. The heat nearly kill them, but I find the plants they want to see. After that they go home to write their books. But while they writing, I think they forget who help them. Au Yong? Who that man?"

While we were talking, a man joined us in the nursery. Au Yong introduced him as Mr. Wu, a local orchid fancier and a good customer and business associate. The two men carried on a brief conversation in Cantonese. When they were finished Mr. Wu shook my hand and left the nursery. Au Yong described his friend in this way: "His passion is orchids. Beautiful collection, but his real business is collecting bad debts. Here in Kuching, no need to call a lawyer. If someone owes you money and won't pay, you call Mr. Wu. When that person gets a phone call about late payment from Mr. Wu, they find money and pay. Before sundown, if possible."

Au Yong continued to discuss his orchid business as his sons repotted plants and brought us cold drinks. "From A to Z . . . I do pollination, set seed, flasking . . . everything. I have no degree in botany, but I am self-taught through observation and this is why I understand orchids. The chief minister of Sarawak, Taib Mahmud, calls me 'the Orchid King,' but still to this day I have no nursery license from the Forestry Department. They tell me I have to prove I am an orchid breeder before issuing license. I show them everything in my nursery—my lab, my seedlings, my mature plants—but still no license. In the meantime, their wives, they all come to me to buy cut flowers for their house. Big armfuls of orchids. They know who I am, but their husbands? They sit in car and look the other way."

I asked Au Yong where his breeding plants came from, and in typical Au Yong fashion he replied, "Don't talk shit to me!

Where you think they come from? They grow in jungle, so I collect in jungle. But I am Buddhist, I am family man. I only collect
very small numbers for breeding and plant division. Like my
own family, I protect the orchid family. I make it grow and this is
my business."

Au Yong described a massive hydroelectric dam under construction at Bakun gorge on the Balui River in the interior of
Sarawak. The reservoir will eventually cover more than 600
square kilometers of former rain forest; the trees have already
been clear-cut from this area. Four thousand people from fifty-
two villages are still awaiting plans for their relocation.

"We can't stop the government from cutting down jungle to
make electricity or start palm oil plantations, just for the sake of
saving orchid and other plants," Au Yong said. "But I ask you,
why CITES law prevent us from saving plants and selling them?
I tell the Forestry Department to open their own orchid nursery
to save these plants if they not let people collect, but they not
interested in salvage operation. Instead they pay money for environmental impact statement and then ten days later big logging
company starts cutting down the whole damn jungle. And
Forestry Department, they the same one who issue CITES
export permit for rare Borneo orchid that grow in Bakun and
other areas. But if I want to send Borneo orchid to other country
I must go to them. Two permits needed—CITES export permit
[to certify that plant is not wild-collected] and phytosanitary
permit [to show it has been inspected for pests and disease]. So I
go to Agriculture Department for 'phyto' permit and they say,
'Let me see CITES permit first.' So then I go to Forestry Department and they say, 'Let me see "phyto" permit first.' Back and
forth I go. From my nursery to Forestry Department it is six
miles. Sometimes I have to make ten trips because officials not

always in office. My customers buy very small number of plants and for only a few plants this is waste of time and waste of money, and what the purpose? They allowing a logging company to kill millions of orchids at Bakun, but they complain about some people just take orchid and put in suitcase and fly out of country. If I get caught mailing orchid without proper permits they can close my nursery. I am Buddhist. I am not afraid to speak my mind and I tell you this all bullshit thinking!"

A year earlier I had brought a small group of orchid growers to Kuching to meet Au Yong. During that visit he had shown us a spectacular *Vanda* orchid in full bloom.

"Very fragrant," Au Yong had said. "We locals call it *tepekang,* but botanical name is *Vanda dearii.*" He lifted the plant toward me, and as he did so, I could hear the sounds of motor drives and camera shutters whirring and clicking like a muted burst of automatic weapon fire.

"Smell!" he said. I put my face near the lush yellow flowers and my nose was immediately bathed in a warm scent of vanilla and cinnamon.

"Nice?" asked Au Yong.

"Very," I replied.

A woman to my left leaned forward to smell the yellow blossoms. As she straightened up she said, "Mmmmm . . . now that's a flower that just makes you want to take your clothes off and roll around on it." Upon hearing this comment, Au Yong's fierce demeanor softened slightly and without a word he looked at me and slowly lifted both eyebrows.

The scented flowers continued to work their olfactory magic on the rest of the group. A man with a luxurious mustache inhaled the fragrance with his eyes closed. As he exhaled I could hear him whisper, "Ahhhhh . . . just like a good woman."

Finally, an elderly little scarecrow of a woman scurried forward. She took a quick sniff of the flower, batted her eyelashes, then rocked back on the heels of her sensible walking shoes and in a breathless, high-pitched voice said, "Wildly . . . sexy."

Au Yong and I laughed at the memory of that afternoon, but it wasn't until my most recent visit in 1998 that Au Yong told me about the time he entered the same plant in the annual Singapore Orchid Show several years earlier. Because of the delicate blossoms, Au Yong decided to carry the plant on his lap during the flight from Kuching to Singapore. This way he knew that the plant would be in perfect condition and at the peak of its bloom when it was displayed. At the Singapore show, several judges and other growers gathered around Au Yong to compliment him on his entry, and based on their comments there was little doubt that this plant would win first prize at the show. Au Yong tried not to let the plant out of his sight, but during the judging contestants are not allowed to be present, and Au Yong had to leave the plant briefly unattended. After the judges had finished making their rounds and evaluating each plant, Au Yong was told that his orchid was disqualified because it had been damaged.

"No! Impossible! Show me the damage!" Au Yong demanded. One of the judges walked back to Au Yong's orchid and pointed out that the pollen sacs were missing from the opened flowers. Au Yong took a look and saw that this was true. At that moment, the old anger that the *bomo* had warned Au Yong about in 1962 began to come back. He could feel the hot coal in his head starting to burn again. The judge was the same one who had taken such a keen interest in the plant just prior to the judging. Au Yong suspected that this man had stolen the pollen to use with his own orchids, and to ensure that a local

Singapore grower would win the prize. Au Yong described what happened next.

"To test him, I put my face up to his face. Close. I tell that judge, 'You steal my pollen!' "

"No, not me. I didn't touch your plant!" said the terrified judge.

"This man, he talk shit to me," said Au Yong. "I know he lie. I see it in his face. If he telling the truth, why he so afraid to look at me? He the pollen thief for sure."

"So what did you do?" I asked.

"I don't do anything," said Au Yong. "I just call Mr. Wu, that his department."

Chapter 8

THE ORCHID JUDGES

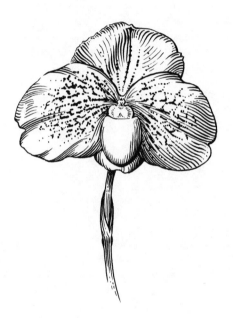

Paphiopedilum greyi Thunder Thighs

Aconfusion of name tags, badges, commemorative lapel pins, and color-coded ribbons were displayed on the chests of a group of very large people. They basked in the damp morning air, seemingly oblivious to the cold concrete floor or the bone-chilling wind that blew through the cavernous space that was once a military warehouse. These people were the orchid judges and they sat at long folding tables eating doughnuts. Many of these men and women had spent more than ten years honing their skills in the fine art of judging the beauty of orchids. Each spring and fall they traveled the U.S. orchid show circuit, moving from city to city, at their own expense, in search of the perfect flower. Orchid judges are not paid for their services and in many ways it is a thankless job. They live in a horticultural twilight zone where the spirit of volunteerism and the pursuit of excellence collide with peer pressure, politics, and the economic needs of commercial orchid growers. Awards mean money and prestige, and an orchid judge's opinion can be a blessing or the kiss of death. The judges at the table had the power to make or break small orchid nurseries, and it was certain that they would do a little of both over the next few hours.

In the distance, a flurry of rodentlike activity was reaching a climax in the exhibition hall as orchid growers put finishing touches on their displays. With the smell of spray paint in the air, they nervously arranged and rearranged black velvet backdrops, removed tissue paper collars from delicate flowers, and paced around in various degrees of high anxiety. One woman, dressed in a brown silk jumpsuit, was wearing a weightlifting belt, purple high-top sneakers, a respirator, and surgical gloves. A tall red-haired man with perfectly creased jeans busied himself staking and twist-tying the flower stalks of his odontoglossums in an attempt to achieve height, symmetry, and beauty through plant bondage. It was all terribly exciting—for the orchid people—and within minutes the judges would be venturing forth to view the displays and collect plants to take back to the judging area. Many of the seasoned orchid show people had already brought their best plants forward for judging.

Once the plants had been selected, they were arranged on a central table that was surrounded by smaller tables where each group of judges would conduct their business. A single plant was placed in the center of each small table, and then, with furrowed brows and a great deal of knuckle cracking and moistening of lips with pink tongues, the judging began. I had never been allowed to sit in on a judging session and it wasn't easy to get permission. But after talking to the president of the local orchid society, the publicist, the hospitality coordinator, various organizers, committee chair people, and the senior judge, I was finally issued a paper badge and given clearance to bear silent witness to the proceedings. I looked forward to listening to the sort of highly esoteric and bewildering insider talk that every niche group develops over time. I anticipated a colorful lexicon of expressions and catchphrases. I was ready for a secret plant language rich in nuance and metaphor.

A hush fell over the table and we sat in silence looking at the first plant. Surrounded by the grim-faced judges, the beautiful, fragile orchid looked naked and vulnerable. No one spoke at first as the judges focused their thoughts and concentrated on the task ahead.

"Nice lip," ventured a student judge nervously.

"I've seen bigger," said one of the accredited judges.

"Big, black, and beautiful, but the bugs been at it," pointed out a third.

"Good gloss, but fatal flaws," chimed in another.

"Cuppy, cuppy," a woman snorted.

"Take it away," mumbled a man across the table, as he went back to eating a chocolate-covered doughnut.

I was seated at a table of very hefty people and the contrast between the large bodies and the diminutive plant was extreme. No one could ever claim that the orchid people are svelte. I found it ironic that these people, who were so utterly different in appearance from the orchids they judge, had spent so many years trying to establish what makes a perfectly formed flower. Huge hands with pudgy, nicotine-stained fingers reached out to caress the delicate blooms in a way that bordered on the obscene. No one wanted to judge the first plant, so it was taken from the table without further comment. Two more plants suffered the same fate before an unusual hybrid caught the judges' interest.

"Well flowered," a woman said grudgingly as the plant was set down.

"LUST-rous dorsal," exclaimed a judge.

"Big one!" agreed another.

"Nice back," said a woman at the end of the table.

"Anyone got a stick?" the senior judge called out.

A man pulled a small centimeter ruler from his shirt pocket and measured the width of the dorsal sepal and also the overall width of the flower from petal tip to petal tip.

"Now that's fat," he concluded, wiping his mouth with the back of his hand. Beads of perspiration began to appear on his forehead.

"Let's do it," someone said, and with that the judges moved in closer. They walked around the table and took turns inspecting the most delicate parts of the flowers as if they were pulling up a little girl's dress. It was impossible to say for sure what they were looking for, but from the sounds of approval I assumed the plant was worthy of their attention.

The flower was carefully measured and then compared with 35-millimeter slides and the vital statistics of the same hybrid from previous American Orchid Society judging sessions. After making their calculations, the judges scribbled on their score sheets. After awarding their points, they added them all up and averaged the total to arrive at the final score. The flower in question had good shape and color, but the overall width was slightly less than the one on file, so it received a lower score, in this case 84 points. A score of 79.5 to 89.49 points earns an Award of Merit (AM), while a score of 89.5 points or more earns a First Class Certificate (FCC). In a year of judging, only a dozen or so flowers win an FCC. There are lesser awards, but for commercial growers and serious hobbyists anything less than an Award of Merit translates into "nice try."

Orchid judges are human. They all have their own aesthetic preferences and hidden agendas and the members of my group were no exception. Despite a uniform judging system, it is inevitable that individual prejudice is part of the equation. This is why one group's Award of Merit could have been the next group's First Class Certificate. Awards determine the market value of a plant and help to establish the reputation of a grower. Overall sales at a show are also affected by judging, so it is easy to understand why the growers get so worked up just prior to these judging events. One disgruntled grower on the orchid show circuit has repeatedly threatened the American Orchid Society with legal action for not judging and awarding his plants.

One of many things that I found interesting about the judging system was that a person can buy a plant minutes before the judging begins, switch the name tag, and enter it in the competition; then if the plant wins an award, the new owner gets to take the credit. If you are a startup commercial nursery this can be a tremendous financial boost and a quick way to establish your credentials with the buying public.

One orchid after another was brought to our table. Before long it became clear that the overall standard of beauty boiled down to a question of big "circular" flowers, bright colors, and bold, showy displays. This fact was made perfectly clear to me when a Chinese *Cymbidium* species was set in front of the judges. The unremarkable-looking plant had a single stalk that held a number of small, mousy-brown, nondescript flowers that were about the size of my thumbnail. After the presentation of a series of stunning hybrids that included one called Thunder Thighs, the little Chinese orchid didn't look very impressive.

"Wham, bam, thank you ma'am," a judge muttered.

"Drop-kick it!" laughed a man at my side.

"*Adios, amigo,*" said doughnut man.

"Oh how cute, but please take it away," said a flannel-and-corduroy-clad behemoth.

"I take it we are all in agreement, gentlemen," said the senior judge.

With that final comment the plant was swept from the table. Next up was another *Paphiopedilum* hybrid that received a mixed reaction.

"Oh, isn't it a joy when you see a bloom like this," the student judge gushed, speaking out of turn.

"Well now!" said a fully accredited judge. "I seriously question the parentage here." He carefully scrutinized the entry card. "No way that this plant is *Paph leopardi* by *makuli*."

"I don't know about that," said a different judge, "but the flower annoys me."

I had no idea how a beautiful flower could be annoying, or what would provoke someone to challenge the parentage of a plant. While the judges vigorously debated these and other fine points I decided to excuse myself from the white-hot center of the orchid judging. The show wouldn't be open to the general public until the next day, so I wandered around the nearly deserted exhibition hall to look at the dozens of orchid displays and sales booths. Eventually I came upon a small corner booth filled with Chinese *Cymbidium* orchids that looked very similar to the one that had been rejected on the judging table.

An elderly Chinese man was moving around the booth arranging shelves that were filled with orchid seedlings offered for sale. As he organized the young plants in neat rows, I noticed the kind expression on his face. When I asked who had grown the plants, he smiled and then placed his hand to his chest to indicate that he was the grower. The man introduced himself as Michael Fung, the owner of Maisie Orchids, a family business that specializes in Chinese *Cymbidium* species as well as Chinese paphiopedilums. He apologized for his poor English and suggested that I wait for his daughter Teresa, who would be returning soon. He assured me that she spoke English well and that she could answer all my questions. While I waited for her I was welcome to look at his orchids.

It wasn't long before I noticed a young Chinese woman with long black hair strolling down the main aisle of the exhibition. She was tall and slender, with fine features. Watching her pause to examine the plants in other booths, I got a sense that this was someone who had spent a lot of time with orchids. Her father introduced us and then went back to his work.

"In China, orchid cultivation and appreciation were a part of the scholar's art for many centuries," Teresa explained. "In Chinese brush painting, cymbidiums have been a well-known theme since the Sung dynasty [960–1279]. Ancient Chinese artists used their individual style to express their feelings through orchid paintings." She gestured to a part of the booth display. "This painting here is a copy of one done by Chang Bian-Kwiu [1693–1765], one of the most prominent brush-painting artists of the Ching dynasty. As a high-ranking officer he was disappointed with the corrupt government, so he resigned and spent the rest of his life brush painting and writing poetry. His favorite theme was orchids."

Teresa showed me one of her favorite orchids: *Cymbidium sinense* variety Faichow Dark. The plant blooms in February, near the Chinese New Year, and it is often associated with that holiday. The small, dark purple flowers were intensely fragrant, giving off a warm, sweet, feminine scent that lured me back to the flowers several times.

"A naughty flower, no?" Teresa said, smiling.

"Like a perfumed dream," I replied. Teresa had the sort of dark, bottomless black eyes that you can fall into if you are not careful.

We moved on to look at what she called a "beginner's cymbidium," *Cymbidium ensifolium,* a trouble-free plant that blooms all summer and through the autumn. Teresa also showed me *Cymbidium kanran,* which produces a spray of more than a dozen dark green, fragrant flowers with delicately patterned lips.

"And these here," Teresa gestured, "are the most graceful ones, *Cymbidium goeringii* variety Chuen Kim. *Chuen kim* means 'spring sword' in Chinese. It blooms in the spring and it is the orchid most commonly seen in traditional Chinese brush painting. And this one is *Cymbidium sinense* variety Jin Wah Shan. It's named for Wah Shan, the very famous mountain in southwest China."

One of the most expensive plants, at $240 for three growths, was *Cymbidium ensifolium alba* variety Golden Threads Ponytail. It wasn't in flower, and I was curious to know why it was five times the price of the other plants. Teresa lightly ran her fingers through the long, thin, variegated leaves and talked about leaf texture, veining, and the subtle details along the leaf margins. She explained that the fragrant flowers were an ivory or light green color, but that the plant was primarily valued for its exquisite foliage. A light wind picked up and in a moment her father was standing beside us, leaning toward the plant. "Ohhh . . . wind blowing through foliage, just look!" he whispered. "This . . . this is beauty, no?"

Leading me to a nearby plant in bloom, Michael pointed out the different parts of the flower. "This we call the nose, here the shoulders, the lip, and the foot." With Teresa translating, Michael told me how some of the orchids in his collection were family heirlooms. They came from plant divisions that had been passed down through the family for more than five hundred years. Listening to these and other stories, all the while inhaling the orchid perfume, it wasn't long before I was completely mesmerized by these two people and their fragrant plants.

For years after this meeting, I wondered if I had received special treatment, until a friend from Hawaii told me what happened the first time he ordered plants from Maisie Orchids. "I resisted adding Chinese cymbidiums to my collection for nearly three years because of lack of space," he explained. "But I finally placed an order. Two weeks after the plants arrived, Teresa called me to see how the orchids (and the new owner) were getting along. Unheard of in the commercial orchid world."

Teresa described the Asian tradition of appreciating orchids for their fragrance, foliage, history, and flower form. The fragrance of Chinese cymbidiums is a delicate combination of jasmine, lily-of-the-valley, and fresh lemon zest. In the tenth century and possibly earlier, wealthy people would travel with an orchid in bloom so that they could enjoy the scent. She also talked about the orchid's "feelings," and how this should dictate what sort of pot to use. At this point I couldn't help thinking how far removed this conversation was from what I had heard at the judge's table an hour earlier. I could not imagine drop-kicking one of these plants, as suggested by one of the judges, and the idea of trying to gauge floral beauty in centimeters now seemed as silly to me as judging the beauty of a woman by measuring the width of her smile or the shape of her ear.

Over the next two days I returned to the Maisie Orchids booth several times to talk to Michael and Teresa about the areas in Yunnan, Guangxi, Guangdong, and Fujian provinces where many of the Chinese cymbidiums grow. We also talked about orchid fragrance. I described a Borneo orchid, *Dendrobium anosmum*, that smells like warm raspberry jam spread on a toasted English muffin (torn, not sliced), and the *Vanda dearii* of Au Yong that produced an aroma of cinnamon, cloves, and vanilla. I asked Teresa if there was a perfume derived from orchids. She told me that the Japanese cosmetic company Shiseido had developed an orchid perfume using Chinese *Cymbidium* species. She didn't know which orchids had been used or what the perfume smelled like, because it was unavailable outside of Japan. Teresa also mentioned that in Japan there was an annual orchid competition based on fragrance. This idea of a fragrance competition immediately caught my interest. I knew that *Dendrobium moniliforme, Cymbidium faberi,* and *Cymbidium kanran* had been used to perfume a special alcove in traditional Japanese homes since ancient times. But the fragrance competition idea struck me as something unique, very Japanese, and an aspect of orchid judging that I wanted to investigate.

After a day of judging and two days of public sales, the orchid show came to an end. The general public was still milling around the parking lot as exhibitors started breaking down their elaborate displays, counting stacks of money, cutting spent blooms, and packing live plants. Large vans moved into the building. The place was filled with the sounds of tape guns sealing cardboard boxes and people calling in pizza orders on their cellular phones. The transformation from floral paradise to demolition site was carried out with a cool efficiency that had been entirely lacking during the setup of the show four days earlier. Cordless electric screwdrivers and socket wrenches reduced the metal-framed structures to orderly piles in a matter of minutes. Metal tubing clattered on the concrete floor and last-minute sales and trades were conducted among the exhibitors. Within hours the huge hall would be empty.

As I walked out to my car, I was surprised to see a dumpster filled with thousands of orchid flowers. Some of them were damaged, but many of the flowers were still fragrant and in good condition. They weren't perfect, but I had no problem gathering dozens of beautiful ones to take with me. The rest of the flowers lay scattered in a heap of chicken bones, hot dog buns, soiled paper plates, beer cans, coffee grounds, and half-eaten spareribs. The garbagemen would arrive the following morning to haul away this elaborate floral display, but by that time the orchid people and the judges would be long gone, headed down the road to the next orchid show.

Chapter 9

THE SCENT OF AN ORCHID

Cymbidium faberi

Jochen Heydel captures fragrance for a living. He is a large, well-groomed man, and his manner is infused with humor and boyish enthusiasm, especially when he starts talking about scent. He is a senior creative perfumer at Bush Boake Allen Americas, a fragrance company located in New Jersey. For more than thirty years the tools of his trade have been his nose and his imagination. When I met Joe in 1997 he was working as a fragrance judge at the Greater New York Orchid Show. Standing in a section of the hall designated for the orchid fragrance competition, we were trying to concentrate on the scent of a flower when a voice immediately behind us cried out: "It is the hand of God . . . the hand of God, I tell you, that has created this beauty!"

Startled, Joe stood bolt upright, turned, and observed an elderly stranger. The man, impeccably attired in a pinstriped blue suit with a crisply starched white dress shirt and a perfectly knotted polka-dot bow tie, was babbling like a street corner zealot cranked up on a breakfast of fortified wine. It became clear that the man was drunk, not on cheap wine, but on the unexpected sight of orchids that filled the entire exhibition space at the World Financial Center in Manhattan.

From what I could gather, he was an office worker who had passed the space empty the previous day, but overnight it had been miraculously transformed into a fragrant paradise filled with thousands of orchids in full bloom. The exhibition hall has a towering glass façade that floods the space with a soft natural light, creating the perfect setting for the largest orchid show in the United States. The man mumbled an apology for his outburst, and then with hands held high as if once again to praise the work of God, he wandered off into the flower-filled hall, where he was soon swallowed up by the foliage. Joe rolled his eyes and shook his head before returning his attention to the little orchid, *Sedirea japonica,* that rested on the table in front of us.

"I don't know anything about orchids," Joe muttered in his pronounced Austrian accent, "but if that man's behavior is any indication of what these plants can do to you, I don't want to know about them. I just study the fragrance and that is as far as I go." Returning to his task, Joe crouched over the orchid, closed his eyes, furrowed his brow, and then inhaled the floral fragrance with short purposeful sniffs. He stepped back to let his nose rest for about five seconds and during this pause I could see his upper lip quivering slightly as a look of intense concentration transformed his face. He then leaned forward to repeat the entire process a second and third time. Joe was quiet for a few moments before describing what he had discovered.

"The first thing that I smell is a citrusy characteristic," he said. "Almost lemony-limey. And right underneath this you can smell jasmine. A very light jasmitic, not the animalic kind of heavy jasmine. And next to this there is something of lily-of-the-valley. The flower also has a slightly woody connotation almost resembling a bit of sandalwood. And that is what I can tell you about *Sedirea japonica.*"

He moved down the table to sniff the flowers of *Cymbidium hoosai* ("roses and violets"), *Coelogyne ochracea* ("sweet and fresh plus heliotrope and roses"), and *Encyclia microbulbon* ("unusual sandalwood notes"). After evaluating the scent from a few more orchids, Joe took a break. He reached into his pocket and pulled out a dry cracker. He took a bite and then put the cracker back in his pocket. Noticing my puzzlement, he explained that he used the cracker to help neutralize his nose.

"It is not possible to go on smelling fragrances endlessly," Joe said. "Eventually your nose will go numb. It's like wine tasting where you have to cleanse your palate from time to time. Some wine tasters use water, others chew bread. People in the perfume world have different techniques for neutralizing their nose. I use a dry cracker, but everyone is different."

Joe described a former colleague who helped him train his nose to detect subtle fragrances. The man was from Poland and he kept a pork-and-garlic sausage in his coat pocket. When he needed to bring his sense of smell back to neutral, he simply reached into his pocket and took a small bite of the sausage. The garlic cleared out all the other scents; only then could the man continue his work.

At the adjoining tables other professional perfumers were busy making their rounds of the different orchids. To our immediate left, Mr. Katsuhiko Tokuda, senior perfumer from Shiseido, the Japanese cosmetic company, was sniffing *Epidendrum parkinsonianum*. This moth-pollinated species is very fragrant at night, but the scent is barely detectable during daylight. With arms held tightly at his sides, Mr. Tokuda leaned toward the flower as if bowing at the waist, but with one foot set in front of the other. He was chewing gum rapidly as he took staccato sniffs from the flowers. He then began to shuffle his feet—slowly at first, but as he picked up the scent he became more animated until he was darting back and forth in front of the flower like a giant besuited insect nervously testing the fragrance.

"You see our friend Mr. Tokuda?" Joe pointed out. "He uses chewing gum to neutralize his nose. He is a legend in the perfume world. Observe the style."

"Ahhh . . . ahhh . . . ahhhhhhhhh!" I could hear Mr. Tokuda muttering to himself with great satisfaction as he bobbed his head in front of the flower. He used his nose like a boxer throwing short tentative jabs, testing, evaluating, gauging, and retesting the scent. Clearly, he was totally absorbed in what his nose was telling him. But then, without warning, the bizarre movements came to an end. "Rose jam, freesia!" he concluded. Mr. Tokuda had solved the fragrance puzzle, and with a sigh of satisfaction he resumed a relaxed, upright posture, scribbled on his score sheet, and then moved to the next orchid, where he repeated the same intense ritual.

While Mr. Tokuda was conducting another of his olfactory dances, I asked Joe to explain what he had meant earlier by a fragrance note being on top of, next to, or beneath another note. "You have to smell through the first thing that hits your nose," Joe told me, "because this is usually the lighter aspect, often a lemony point. It is the most volatile component. The different notes or aspects reveal themselves in stages, and you have to smell through them to get to the bottom of the fragrance puzzle. There are top, middle, and base notes, and that is how we describe fragrances. If you open a bottle of perfume, what is in the neck of the bottle is what hits you first. This is the top note. Then you put the fragrance on your skin and let it evaporate for about ten seconds, which gets you to the middle notes. After perhaps an hour you get to the bottom notes. The base notes are the least volatile and they come up last. We use the same criteria for evaluating and understanding the scent of orchids or any other sort of flower."

We moved on to *Cymbidium linearisepalum,* where Joe once again broke down the scent into its component parts. "Well, here the first thing that hits you is not a citrus note, but jasmine . . . jasmine album. A very light, extremely elegant jasmine note. And right after that it goes over into lily-of-the-valley (known in the trade as *muguet*), which is very fresh. Not citrusy fresh, but a fresh floral scent. I also smell apple blossoms, and now here is something interesting." He took another sniff. "There is a note that reminds me of peaches. Yes, fresh peaches, slightly warmed in the sun. Very nice. So you have these four things: jasmine, lily-of-the-valley, apple blossoms, and fresh peaches. The peach part is interesting because it fits nicely with the jasmine and the lily-of-the-valley. Because of this fit, I think of the flower as almost having a finished fragrance, a naturally balanced blend which is quite unusual."

Part of the difficulty of comparing and judging orchid fragrances has to do with the fact that most flowers follow a fragrance cycle that makes them smell differently throughout the day. For example, *Catasetum expansum* smells like an industrial floor cleaner before noon, and like dill seed and rye bread later in the day. *Clowesia rosea* has a scent of menthol mid-morning, but by the afternoon it smells like cinnamon rolls.

During a short break, I learned that none of the five judges raised orchids and that their primary interest was to study the flowers for new scents or combinations of scents. They were looking for inspiration, but they also talked about fragrance memory, which is the ability to conjure up past events or emotions based on smell. Vanilla was given as a common example of how fragrance memory works.

"Whose memory is not stimulated by the scent of vanilla?" asked Joe. "The fragrant vanilla bean is really just the cured seed capsule of *Vanilla planifolia,* an orchid that comes from Central America, the West Indies, and Mexico. The bean was used by the Aztecs to flavor a chocolate drink, and by the early sixteenth century vanilla was being used as a perfume in Europe. Most people associate vanilla with ice cream, cakes, and cookies, but the substance has continued to be important in the perfume world. Without the scent of vanilla, Jacques Guerlain could never have created the lush and sensual perfumes Jicky and Shalimar. Vanilla has always been thought to be an aphrodisiac, and there might be something to this claim, because it is found in most good perfumes."

Before the judges went back to evaluating the orchids, Joe introduced me to Mr. Tokuda. When I told him I had heard that Shiseido had developed a perfume based on Chinese cymbidiums, he bowed modestly and said that the name of the perfume was Tentatrice and that he had worked on the project. Mr. Tokuda told me the perfume was not available outside of Japan, but if I would come to the corporate office of Shiseido the following day he would be happy to discuss his work with orchid fragrance and let me sample the orchid-inspired perfume Tentatrice.

Early the following morning, at the Shiseido office on Third Avenue, Mr. Tokuda and I sat at opposite ends of a massive and highly polished black marble conference table that must have weighed several tons. Yasushi Kunii, vice president in charge of corporate planning, was there along with several assistants. At Mr. Tokuda's end of the table there was a three-inch-thick pile of research documents and lab reports detailing his work with orchid fragrance. In a separate stack he had organized a copy of the official Japanese guidelines for judging orchid fragrance (based on intensity, elegance, gorgeousness, and freshness) and a signed book of poetry that he had written (in Japanese). Set slightly off to one side was an exquisitely wrapped parcel that contained a very large bottle of Tentatrice.

Mr. Tokuda began the conversation by describing how the Japanese divide orchids into two basic groups. The first group, *To-yo-ran,* commonly known as Oriental orchids, are from Taiwan, Japan, China, or Korea. These orchids bear small, highly fragrant flowers; the plants have been collected and admired for their foliage and scent since ancient times. The second group, *Yo-ran,* are the ones that were introduced from European and other Western countries after 1868, when the Westernization of Japan started.

"For us there is a very clear distinction between Western-style orchids and Oriental-style orchids. In America, people tend to commingle' orchids. Americans appreciate orchids primarily for their color, shape, and big size. They hybridize any orchid to get something new, and, please excuse me, but these flowers can look very manipulated and unnatural. For *To-yo-ran* orchids we put emphasis on fragrance, leaves, the container, and the potting mix. It is the overall presentation, not just the big flower on top. When you look at the *To-yo-ran* orchids you know that the flowers are not so appealing by themselves. It is all about understatement and balance and this is how we appreciate orchids."

Mr. Tokuda described the Japanese tradition of using fragrant *To-yo-ran* orchids to perfume their homes. The orchids are placed in the *tokonoma,* which is a slightly raised alcove in the formal room of a Japanese house. This alcove is the aesthetic focal point of the room and it is where calligraphic scrolls and flower arrangements are placed. The *tokonoma* is frequently used as a stage on which to represent the different seasons, and the orchids most commonly displayed in this area are *Cymbid-*

ium faberi and *C. kanran,* as well as *Dendrobium moniliforme, Neofinetia falcata* (described as smelling like lily-of-the valley by day and butter cookies by night), and *Calanthe izu-insularis,* which has an intense fragrance of daphne.

Tentatrice, a French word meaning "temptress" or "seducer," was designed to capture the allure of *To-yo-ran* orchids. When Mr. Tokuda explained that the name of the perfume was not his idea, a Japanese woman laughed politely behind her hand and the other gentlemen at the conference table chortled modestly in response. Then the room fell silent and Mr. Tokuda described the perfume as a bouquet of jasmine and lily-of-the-valley, with oakmoss, musk, and amber notes, combined with methyl epijasmonate.

Methyl epijasmonate ($C_{13}H_{20}O_3$) didn't sound very sexy to me, but it is the chemical compound responsible for the warm, intoxicating feminine scent of Chinese cymbidiums. The Shiseido research laboratories in Yokohama isolated methyl epijasmonate from *Cymbidium faberi;* it is one of the important building blocks that Mr. Tokuda used to create Tentatrice.

Mr. Tokuda launched into a detailed description of how to capture orchid fragrance and analyze the results by using headspace technology, gas chromatography, and mass spectrometry. He spoke passionately about the fine art of organoleptic evaluations of scent accomplished by sniffing the exit port of a Hitachi Model 163 gas chromatograph outfitted with an effluent splitter set at a 1-to-10 ratio. This was far more than I wanted to know about the mechanics of capturing the scent of an orchid. But what I found interesting about the technology was the fact that it made it possible to isolate, measure, and identify the aromatic components released by the flowers. When we put our nose close to an orchid flower we smell volatilized molecules released into the air in hopes of attracting a pollinating insect. The scent of an orchid flower often contains anywhere from 100 to 200 different chemical components, and when the floral vapors are viewed on a gas chromatograph paper printout, it becomes clear that what we are smelling is a complex swirl of molecules, sometimes on the order of one-100,000th of a gram each. The way in which these minute concentrations are charted on the graph is called the fragrance fingerprint.

Once the component parts of the fragrance fingerprint have been identified and synthesized, a master perfumer like Mr. Tokuda or Jochen Heydel can get to work on the more difficult task of selecting the bits and pieces that will evoke the fragrance memory of a flower like *Cymbidium faberi*. It is the delicate balance of ingredients working in conjunction with memory that makes a perfume work, and once a person has experienced the scent of fragrant orchids wafting through a traditional Japanese house on a warm day, it is easy to understand the allure of Tentatrice. When I asked Mr. Tokuda why the perfume was not sold in the United States or Europe, he told me that it was a fragrance that Westerners might not understand. "It is very subtle and light and in a crowd of people it might not be noticed. It was specifically designed for the Japanese domestic market, and just like our preference for *To-yo-ran* orchids, we have our own sort of perfume preference. Orchids are designed to attract a certain insect, and each flower sends out a fragrance message to attract that insect. The other insects do not understand the message from the flower. In the same way, Tentatrice sends out a fragrance message for a certain type of person. The other people do not react, because they do not understand the message."

Chapter 10

PERFUMED LEGS
AT THE OYSTER BAR

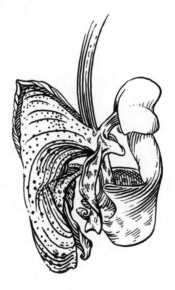

Coryanthes speciosa

I met Sandro Cusi in a cafeteria near Battery Park while he was attending the New York Orchid Show as an exhibitor and speaker. By this time I had developed a special interest in the pollination strategy of the Mexican bucket orchid, *Coryanthes speciosa,* and because Sandro is an orchid grower from Mexico, I thought he would be a good person to talk to about the plant. But first I wanted to know how Sandro had become involved with orchids.

"It was a long time ago," he said. "At least thirty years. There was an old plant collector who used to come to the open-air flower market in Mexico City. He sold cactus and orchids and his name was Teódulo Chávez. He was an Indian and he was already an old man when I first met him. Teódulo was one of those rare, soft-spoken experts. He was money-poor, but he loved plants, he loved people, and he loved life. The sort of person we don't see much of anymore. He had collected plants for some very famous people when he was younger."

"Which famous people?" I asked.

"Well, probably you have heard of Diego Rivera, the muralist. Diego loved orchids. Teódulo collected for him and showed him how to take care of the plants. Teódulo was very particular about who he sold his plants to. If they didn't know how to grow them he wouldn't sell, because it is an easy thing to kill an orchid. The other person was Leon Trotsky. Trotsky adored cactus. He had a passion for them and after Stalin forced him into exile he had plenty of spare time to devote to his cactus collection."

"It must have been a fairly short-lived hobby for Trotsky," I said, "considering his brief stay in Mexico before being assassinated."

"Yes. A brief, passionate interest," Sandro said. "But this is really not such a bad thing in life, is it?"

Sandro described how Teódulo taught him many things, the first of which was how to make an old Aztec drink known as agave pulque. Teódulo told him that to the north of Mexico City there were many arid places, and in those places the Indians drank a lot of pulque. They drank it instead of water.

"It is slimy, acidic like buttermilk, slightly alcoholic, and it can be mixed with fruit," Sandro explained. "The god of pulque is worshiped in that area and Teódulo told me all about it. We went there, we drank the pulque, and later he told me about orchids."

Teódulo became Sandro's mentor. The apprenticeship lasted for many years and it involved countless journeys into remote jungle areas to learn how different orchids grow in the wild. Teódulo was not the sort of plant collector who just took plants out of the jungle to sell in the market. He studied them, and from years of observation he understood the secrets of every orchid he collected. Teódulo also knew the behavior of the pollinating insects of the different orchids, as well as the exact conditions under which the plants would thrive. He only collected select examples of different orchid species and emphasized that it was better to divide good plants and grow them in a nursery than to harvest wild plants continuously for a quick profit. Over time, he passed on to Sandro his philosophy of collecting and his knowledge of cultivating orchids.

Teódulo specialized in *Laelia* orchids, which are related to cattleyas. Their flowers are slightly less showy than most cattleyas, but they grow on trees, where they flower in great profusion. Teódulo's wife sold laelias and other orchids during the flowering season at the Friday market in Coyoacán, which is located in the southern part of Mexico City. Many of Teódulo's plants won awards at the local orchid society, but this sort of recognition never affected his attitude toward the orchids. He was a plant hunter in pursuit of a very limited number of new and exotic species. He carried a small collecting bag, and when it was full it was time to go home.

"Teódulo was also a devout Catholic," Sandro told me. "At the beginning of each day, and whenever we would come upon a good group of plants, he would make the sign of the cross and thank God for the continuing health of the orchids. Now most of these areas are unrecognizable because of clearing for agriculture and the work of the charcoal makers."

Teódulo didn't care too much about growing orchids, or selling them. What he loved was to be out collecting. Sandro told me how the old man would sometimes come to live with his family for a week or two at a time. Teódulo would be so excited that he could not sleep the night before they would go out looking for orchids, and Sandro often found his friend sitting by the edge of the patio in the middle of the night. With his little collecting sack by his side, the old man would sit on a stool and quietly wait for the sunrise.

Teódulo would also tell Sandro's children stories about his plant-collecting adventures. One of those stories had to do with the time the police took Teódulo from his home in the middle of the night. "At that time," Sandro explained, "when the police came for you at night, your family would never see you again.

But three days later Teódulo returned home, barefoot and tired but with some money."

"*¡Qué milagro!*" his wife had cried at the sight of Teódulo.

"That crazy Trotsky," Sandro explained, "it was all his doing. He was so worried about people knowing his movements and following him that one day when he decided to go collecting cactus and some orchids for Diego's wife, Frida Kahlo, he just had Teódulo snatched from his home with no explanation."

One day, not long before Teódulo died, he and Sandro and a few friends were in the forest looking for new plants. Teódulo could no longer walk very well, but his eyesight was still quite good and he spotted an orchid high in a tree. It was in flower and so of course Teódulo wanted to climb the tree to have a closer look.

"We hadn't been drinking pulque," Sandro said. "He just wanted to climb that tree and it was very tall. We stood beneath him expecting him to fall at any moment, but Teódulo, he knew how to climb a tree. It took him a long time but he finally got to the orchid. He stayed at the top of the tree studying the orchid before he dropped it to us and climbed down."

The plant was a beautiful example of *Cuitlauzina pendula*. Teódulo had taken his time at the top of the tree to carefully examine the color, size, and form of the flowers, making sure that they were perfect, before collecting the plant. By the time he reached the ground, Teódulo was covered in dirt and tree bark, and the ants had bitten his neck and legs, but he had a wonderful smile on his face. Sandro described how the old man sat at the foot of the tree holding the orchid in his hands and displaying the cascades of shell-pink blooms for everyone to see. The flowers gave off a sweet fragrance, similar to orange blossoms, and Teódulo introduced the orchid to the other people as if he were describing an old friend.

"I have climbed the tree!" Teódulo said. "In my eightieth year I have climbed a tree for this beautiful orchid." A few months later he passed away.

Sandro and I sat in the New York cafeteria drinking coffee. Snow flurries swirled outside and I listened to stories about Sandro's other journeys into the tropical forests of Mexico. There was no rush to get back to the exhibit and eventually the conversation came around to the Mexican bucket orchid, *Coryanthes speciosa.*

Bucket orchids are epiphytes, and they are found growing on trees in the wet tropical forests of Mexico, Central America, and South America. The flowers emerge in clusters, and at the base of each flower there is a small bucket, which is how the plant got its name. What makes bucket orchids unique is the complex relationship they have developed with their pollinating insect. It is an excellent example of coevolution and this is what originally stimulated my interest in *Coryanthes speciosa.*

Both Sandro and I were also intrigued by the plight of the insect pollinator, the male euglossine bee. Sandro, being the Latin gentleman that he is, pointed out the similarities to human courtship. There was an ardent suitor, tantalizing promises, a noble quest, intoxicating perfumes, dancing, deception, hope, betrayal, adventure, courage, and, in the end, hard-earned knowledge gleaned from bitter experience. The entire scenario is orchestrated by a flower for the sole purpose of enticing an insect into transporting pollen from one blossom to another. This is how it works.

By the time the flower opens (often with an audible popping

sound), two specialized glands have already started to secrete a clear, colorless liquid that drips into the bottom of the bucket and forms a small reservoir. The flowers now begin to produce an intoxicating perfume that proves irresistible to the metallic green male euglossine bee. But, as Sandro pointed out, the fragrance does not come from the fluid dripping into the bucket. The droplets serve a different purpose entirely.

Within minutes of the flower's blooming, male bees, responding to the orchid's scent, start to swarm around the flower in a state of great agitation. They hover, seeking a foothold on the mesochile, a tubular part that connects the bucket to the rest of the flower. Grasping at the slippery surface of this erect and curving vertical shaft, the excited bees collect a waxy perfume from just below a bonnet-shaped structure called the hypochile.

The bees continue to hover and land while using the hairs on their front legs to transfer the aromatic substance to their middle legs and then to special pockets located in the hind tibiae. This procedure is repeated several times until the bee has properly perfumed himself. The perfume is not a type of sugary nectar generally associated with the common honeybee. It is a special potion that the bee will use to attract females during his exotic courtship dance. Different species of *Coryanthes* attract different species of bees because each male bee needs to have a very specific sort of scent. Only after the male bee has collected enough perfume is he ready to fly off in search of a mate.

Because of the mad rush to get at the limited amount of special scent, many male bees converge on the same flower. The flowers stay in bloom for only a few days, and as a result, there can be a considerable amount of shoving with the middle legs, head butting, and jostling for position beneath the hypochile. Occasionally, one of the bees either loses his footing on the slippery surface of the shaft or gets knocked into the bucket when his wings collide with a droplet from the dripping gland.

Once inside the bucket, there is only one exit—a narrow tunnel that leads through the front wall of the flower to daylight and freedom. Just below the entrance to the tunnel there is a step on the inside wall of the bucket. The sodden bee uses this step to climb out of the fluid and into the narrow passageway. The bee must wiggle and squeeze his way forward, stopping to rest many times, as there is no room to turn around or back out. Just before he reaches daylight he passes beneath two paired masses of pollen (the pollinia) attached to the roof of the tunnel. At that precise moment the pollinia disengage and become fixed to the spot on the bee's back where the thorax and abdomen are hinged. By the time the bee has climbed free of the tunnel, the pollen is attached between his wings like a small backpack. His ordeal may have taken as long as forty-five minutes.

Wet and disoriented, the bee pauses to dry himself on the winglike lateral sepals. Once the pollen has been collected, the flower has served its purpose, the scent vanishes, and the flower quickly wilts. It may be a day or more before perfume from a second bucket orchid will arouse the bee's interest.

For *Coryanthes speciosa* to be pollinated, a bee carrying the pollinia must fall into the same floral obstacle course a second time. The chances of this happening are remote and consequently pollination occurs infrequently. On the bee's visit through a second bucket orchid, a catch mechanism on the roof of the escape tunnel seizes the pollen backpack. By this time the pollen has dried and diminished in size so that it will fit nicely into the stigmatic surface. In this way the bucket orchid is pollinated and, with luck, a seed pod will form.

The male bee may have been used by the flower, but hopefully he has also collected what he needs—the waxy perfume for his legs. Freed of his backpack, and remembering his own procreative duties, he flies off to a display site, where he dances and conducts an intricate flight and buzz pattern. Fancy footsteps are performed as a heady scent of perfume wafts from his hind legs. With this kind of action going on, what female bee can possibly resist the temptation to land and get better acquainted?

When I asked Sandro if he knew of a good place to see *Coryanthes speciosa* growing in the wild, he told me it was a common plant in southern Mexico and that the best time to find it in bloom was during the summer months of June and July. The plant grew in the jungle at many points along the Río Usumacinta, which flows between the state of Chiapas in Mexico and Guatemala. Sandro assured me that if one did not mind sleeping in a hammock for a few nights in the small riverside villages, eating food from the markets and roadside stalls, and traveling with the local boatmen, the plant would not be too difficult to find. A round trip from Mexico City should take no more than ten days.

Sandro mentioned one special place at the headwaters of a jungle tributary, not far from the partially excavated Mayan ruins at Yaxchilán. He had been to this *Coryanthes* habitat many years earlier. He called the place El Ostional—the Oyster Bar. The name comes from a delectable freshwater bivalve that inhabits a stretch of rocky shoreline. It is a remote place, about three hours by boat from the nearest village. The jungle overhangs a quiet swimming hole at a bend in the river. It sounded like a wonderful journey and Sandro and I made plans to go there the following summer. He needed a division of the plant, and this would give me a perfect opportunity to visit the habitat of *Coryanthes speciosa* and watch the euglossine bees hard at work.

But the summer went by without a visit to the Oyster Bar. Both Sandro and I were busy working on other projects. Two years later, when we were both free to make the journey, the place was no longer safe for orchid hunters or strangers. Smugglers and drug traders operating between Guatemala and Mexico were using the small tributaries along the Río Usumacinta, and when Sandro heard that people had been shot in the area, he phoned to tell me that we would have to postpone our trip again. It might be years before we go to the Oyster Bar to look for *Coryanthes speciosa*, but I am content to wait until the time is right. Meanwhile I continue my friendship with Sandro, pursue my growing interest in agave pulque, and listen to stories about the great orchid hunter Teódulo Chávez.

Chapter 11

ON THE ROAD
WITH DR. BRAEM

Paphiopedilum supardii

It was just before midnight on a cool summer evening when the night train from Paris pulled into Frankfurt station. Standing beneath a dim light on the train platform, half obscured by shadow, was Dr. Guido Jozef Braem. I could see the red glow of a cigarette that he held in one hand. Several people had described this man to me as an international orchid smuggler. Others, including many distinguished botanists and commercial orchid growers, regarded him as a brilliant scientist and conservationist. Whoever the man might be, he looked quite sinister standing alone in the partial light. All that was lacking was a trench coat, a fedora with the brim pulled low over his face, and perhaps a few rare orchids stuffed up his trouser legs and taped to his ankles.

Over the previous months we had talked on the phone several times, but apart from his booming voice and strong opinions on every possible topic, I had very little idea what to expect of Dr. Braem. He had sent me a copy of his curriculum vitae and his publications list, which I found quite impressive, if not a bit intimidating. The document ran to nine pages; the items listed included a Ph.D. on the taxonomy of *Oncidium* orchids of the Caribbean, as well as details of extensive work in the fields of plant morphology, cytogenetics, population ecology, biochemistry, and numerical taxonomy. He was the editor and publisher of *Schlechteriana* (a German orchid journal), a contributing editor to the *Pleurothallid Alliance* (whatever that might be) *Newsletter,* and the scientific editor of the Italian publication *Orchids.* Each year he lectured worldwide on conservation issues, orchid cultivation, and the fine points of orchid taxonomy. Dr. Braem also made regular visits to the most important orchid habitat sites on earth in order to take photographs of rare plants and to collect scientific data on how they grow in their native habitats. He is fluent in English, Dutch, French, and German, and is the author of more than one hundred scientific articles and six books. His most recent publication, *The Genus Paphiopedilum: Natural History and Cultivation,* is co-authored by Charles and Margaret Baker. Dr. Braem is widely acknowledged as a world authority on *Paphiopedilum* species, and has also contributed significantly to the scientific knowledge of orchids by identifying and describing more than a dozen new species. Reading over Dr. Braem's curriculum vitae, I was struck with how little it resembled the background of an international plant thief. But by this time I took nothing for granted when it came to dealing with the orchid people.

On Norris Powell's recommendation, Dr. Braem had agreed to talk to me about the orchid trade. His only condition was that we meet in person, and this is why I had come to Frankfurt. To my surprise, Dr. Braem had also offered to take me to several orchid greenhouses in Germany, Belgium, and Holland and introduce me to nurserymen who had been raided in recent years. He wanted me to hear their stories firsthand, and inspect the relevant court papers and other supporting documents in order to understand what had happened to them.

The train jolted to a stop, the glass doors slid open with a blast of compressed air, and I stepped onto the platform. A cool wind blew flurries of grit into my face as I approached the lone figure standing by the light.

"Dr. Braem, I presume?"

"Yeah, that is me," he replied, pumping my hand with a vigorous handshake. "Who the hell else do you think would be standing out here in the middle of the night? Now let's get in the bloody car."

Early the following morning we set off on a road journey that would eventually take us through northern Germany, Holland, and parts of Belgium. Our first destination was the orchid nursery of Mr. Nebojsha "Bosha" Popow, one of the finest and most controversial growers of *Paphiopedilum* orchid species in Europe. It was a three-hour drive, during which Dr. Braem and I began our conversation about scientific research, the orchid trade, and smuggling.

Part of me had been expecting a cantankerous, dry, and opinionated botanist whose conversation would rarely venture far beyond the realm of floral bracts and staminoidal shield morphology. Well, I was right about the opinionated bit, but as it turned out Dr. Braem had a wide range of interests that included archeology and European history; chess; the eighteenth-century British botanist Joseph Banks, who had accompanied Captain Cook on the HMS *Endeavour;* and the giant carnivorous pitcher plants of Southeast Asia. He proved to be an excellent traveling companion. I soon discovered that his passion for orchids was equaled by his knowledge of the fine beers of Belgium, many of which we sampled during our leisure time over the next five days.

"So, you want to know why people call me an orchid smuggler?" Dr. Braem asked, as we pulled onto the Autobahn. "Well, you had better get your tape recorder running so that you get the bloody story straight." For the next couple of hours Dr. Braem talked about his experiences as an international orchid smuggler.

"First, you must understand that the everyday customs officers in Germany, and elsewhere, who are assigned the task of enforcing the CITES plant regulations and conservation laws would have a very hard time distinguishing between a blade of grass and a palm tree. They have no botanical training whatsoever. So, what happened to me in 1986 is this: I was preparing for my book on paphiopedilums, but there was some controversy and debate over a particular plant called *Cypripedium schmidtianum*. And so I decided to have a look at the original type specimen of the flower, which happens to reside in a jar of alcohol in Denmark. The specimen was collected by Koontling in 1905 on the island of Koh Chang off the coast of Thailand. Anyway, a colleague of mine at the Botanical Museum in Copenhagen was kind enough to pack up the bottle with the dead pickled flower and send it to my address in Germany. Well, the thing got stuck at the customs office nearby and so I had to go there to get it."

The first problem was that because it was a dead flower from a botanical institution, no one had thought of getting a CITES permit for the thing. And since the flower was on loan to Dr. Braem for research purposes, no one had included a bill or an invoice with the shipment. So the customs officer charged Dr. Braem with a CITES offense, saying he was smuggling a protected orchid into Germany. Dr. Braem tried to explain that it was his understanding that the rules only applied to live plant material. But the officer said that he didn't care if it was a live orchid, a dried orchid, a pickled orchid, or a candied orchid, because his book of CITES regulations said "orchid." There was no distinction between live and dead plants. The other thing they charged him with was tax evasion, because there was no invoice. When Dr. Braem explained to the officer that a colleague had sent him the dead orchid specimen to study for free and that he would be sending the specimen back to him, the officer yelled, "There is nothing for free in this world and I don't believe you!" Dr. Braem simply wanted to study the flower for his book, and all of a sudden he found himself with this idiot in a uniform telling him that he was an orchid smuggler and a tax cheat.

"What did you do?" I asked.

"Well," Dr. Braem laughed, "as you can imagine, after an hour of arguing with this moron without getting anywhere, I found the situation very frustrating. I took a deep breath and tried to calm myself down because I knew that if I lost my temper with this sort of man it would only make things worse. I thought about what he had said and tried to understand his point of view and accept the fact that he was only enforcing the rules as they had been written. *Surely, there must be some simple solution*, I told myself. I really just wanted to get on with my work. I was considering my options when I looked up and noticed the customs officer smirking at me. He knew he had me by the balls. I didn't like his attitude, so I just leaned over the counter and punched him in the face. He hit the floor like a sack of potatoes."

"And then?"

"Well, I have to admit I felt pretty good, but only for a few moments. This is Germany and you can imagine what happened next. The whole place was swarming with armed guards. They went crazy. A lot of yelling, people running around; and during this confusion I made it out the door, climbed in my car, and drove home. Of course they knew where to find me, and it wasn't long before I was charged with assaulting a civil servant (which is a very serious offense in Germany), orchid smuggling, and tax evasion."

In Germany, cases like this are sometimes settled out of court by the judge, who can request that a donation be paid to a charity of his choice, and this is what happened to Dr. Braem. In the end, the charges were dropped and he paid 800 deutschmarks (DM) to the local Red Cross, which he didn't mind in the slightest.

"And what happened to the pickled orchid?" I asked.

"Maybe two months expired between my little encounter with the customs officer and the payment of the fine. After that they sent the orchid specimen back to Denmark. I ended up having to get in my car and drive to Copenhagen to see the flower, which, as it turned out, was nothing more than a flower of *Paphiopedilum callosum*. I had to laugh at this. All this hassle just to look at a pickled specimen in order to confirm that *Cypripedium schmidtianum* is a synonym of *Paphiopedilum callosum*."

Dr. Braem's second experience as a smuggler took place in 1990, while he was working on a book about cypripedium orchids. He needed to look at some dead orchid specimens stored in the Reichenbach Herbarium at the Natural History Museum in Vienna. Dr. Harald Riedle, the director there, told him, "No problem, Guido, you don't have to come to Vienna, we will mail the specimens to you." And of course the shipment was seized at customs and Dr. Braem was once again charged with smuggling orchids. This matter also ended up in court. The specimens from the Reichenbach Herbarium were collected between 1810 and 1890. One particular specimen had been dried in 1822, long before the unification of Germany and the creation of the modern border with Austria.

In court Dr. Braem was charged with trading protected species of orchids. To most people, the term "trade" suggests a commercial transaction, but as the CITES law is written, trade is simply the transport of any orchid across international borders. So once again Dr. Braem was an orchid smuggler. This second case was also settled out of court, and it cost Dr. Braem 2,000 DM, which went to the Children's Cancer Hospital in the nearby town of Giessen. Dr. Braem thinks the hospital a very worthwhile institution, but he would have preferred to make the donation under different circumstances.

This was not the end of the story. The specimens were confiscated, and, by German law, confiscated material becomes the property of the state of Germany. So Dr. Riedle had to get the Austrian government to intervene on behalf of the Reichenbach Herbarium to get the orchid specimens back.

"Did you ever get to see the plants?" I asked.

"Oh yes, but in Vienna," Dr. Braem said. "The whole thing took six months. It cost me 2,000 DM for the fine, another 1,500 DM for my lawyer, then there was the flight to Vienna, the hotel, meals, booze, and all the rest. The whole thing ended up costing me between 5,500 and 6,000 DM, and all this because of how the CITES laws are written. The law reads no trade in 'plants, or parts thereof, or products thereof.' It doesn't stipulate that the plant has to be alive. So this makes me an orchid smuggler."

In the CITES regulations there is a provision that allows for trade in orchid specimens for science and education, but only between scientific institutions. Independent researchers are excluded. The necessary document is known as a Scientific CITES. It is interesting to note that CITES officials are also the ones who have absolute control over which institutions are "bona fide" and can obtain Scientific CITES to import plants for study. According to Dr. Braem, in many countries this "bona fide" status is granted without official guidelines for qualification or even a formal application process. In this way a very small group of people manage to control who can gain legal access to the plant material.

"If you want to work with orchids," Dr. Braem told me, "these kinds of rules force you to break the law. You have to become a criminal in order to continue your work. But of course the rules are not applied equally. If you work at a well-connected and politically powerful institution, nobody would ever question a shipment of live or dead plants. The rest of us, if we want specimens, we are forced to throw the things in the trunks of our cars and drive across the border. This sort of preferential treatment does not help conserve orchids or help in the study of these plants."

According to an independent botanist from Denmark who has collaborated with Kew, a package bearing the stamp of the Royal Botanic Gardens, or which is being sent to Kew, passes international borders like a diplomatic pouch, with no questions asked. But when this same botanist wanted to exchange plant material with other scientists, he often found it difficult or impossible to do so. It is the cherished goal of every botanist to name a new species, and so with this sort of double standard being applied it is easy to comprehend why many scientists are upset. Botanists at Kew have claimed that they do not receive preferential treatment, and that they must apply for CITES permits just like everyone else.

Dr. Braem went on to explain how the orchid trade laws in Germany are very complicated. There are the federal laws, regional laws, plus the 1973 Washington Convention to adhere to. They are all slightly different, and for each of these laws there are regulations on how to interpret the law and how to enforce it. So the end result is that very few lawyers, let alone botanists or commercial growers, can understand the laws, which themselves are in a state of perpetual metamorphosis. Even lawyers in Europe and the United States who specialize in these laws say that it is nearly impossible to make sense of the contradictory regulations.

"The CITES people in Germany are the ones that are supposed to know what it is all about," Dr. Braem said, "and after my Vienna incident I wanted to know precisely how to legally receive scientific plant specimens from across international borders. I called the CITES authorities at the Ministry of Environment in Bonn, and I talked to Dr. Emmons, who was at the time the highest-ranking official on environmental issues. I asked him about CITES regulations regarding dried herbarium specimens, and his response was very concise and simple. He said, 'What is a herbarium specimen?' 'Aren't you a botanist?' I asked him. 'No,' the man replied, 'I am a lawyer. I have no idea what a herbarium specimen is.'

"So now you see what the scientific community is up against," said Dr. Braem. "The people who are running the show just don't know what they are doing when it comes to orchids and other plants. It is the opinion of many scientists that the real intention of these regulations is to slow things down so that people just throw up their hands and give up and walk away."

I asked Dr. Braem if there was a way for him to get his orchid specimens without ending up in court. "Oh sure, there is a way, and this is what me and my colleague have to do. The German customs people use a book called *A Dictionary of the Flowering Plants and Ferns,* by J. C. Willis, as their bible for identifying plant species. Never mind that the book is several decades out of date, never mind that many of the orchid species names are no longer valid, and never mind that it is not even a taxonomic book that is recognized by botanists. The customs people like this book, so we have to use it just to stay out of trouble. And of course the customs officers always want a bill or invoice so that they can charge tax. I have to make up a fake bill for 40 or 50 DM for each shipment so that the customs people can charge me 27 percent tax. This makes them happy, I get to do my work, and I have my peace and quiet. This way I avoid being called an orchid smuggler, but on the other hand, I am forced to apply for plants under incorrect names, pay customs duties that I don't owe, and then sign false documents to get the plants through customs. In the end, what serious scientist is going to play this game? Many of us just don't bother anymore. There are plenty of ways to get around the rules. This is not the way that people in the scientific community prefer to get their plant material, but this is what happens."

Dr. Braem explained that the big German CITES crackdown on orchids and other rare plants took place around 1981. At that time, the German government reversed the burden of proof of plant ownership so that it was up to the orchid grower or botanist to prove that he or she had possession of the plant before 1981. If, for example, a person or business has had a plant of the Borneo orchid species *Paphiopedilum roth-schildianum* since, let's say, 1963, customs officers can demand to see documents verifying this fact. There were no such documents in 1963, but this does not bother CITES officials or customs officers. In lieu of such proof they are quite happy to confiscate the plants in question.

As recently as 1993, an official CITES export permit, issued by a state government in Malaysia, was rejected by U.S. customs officials in Seattle because the legally signed and stamped document was printed on the "wrong sort of paper." The shipment, a boxful of Borneo orchids, died in custody while the paperwork was reprocessed on the "right sort of paper." It is common for CITES export permits from orchid-producing countries like Indonesia, India, and Thailand to be singled out as forgeries by customs officials in Europe and the United States. If customs officials say your plants are illegal or your paperwork is not genuine, they have your property confiscated and you are just out of luck. You have the option of going to court, but in practice people just abandon the plants because of the time and expense involved, and because the plants will die before they can reclaim them.

The more Dr. Braem talked about German and international regulations governing the orchid trade, the more animated he became and the more pressure he applied to the accelerator of his car. By the time the speedometer needle was touching 200 kilometers per hour, I had tightened my shoulder harness and Dr. Braem had moved on to a general condemnation of CITES.

"Anyone who says that CITES is a law to protect species is wrong. CITES, as it is being enacted, is a law to destroy species. And this is because if you cannot or will not, for whatever reason, protect the natural environment where those species are found, there should be no talk about the legality or illegality of taking a few plants from that environment and putting them into cultivation."

Dr. Braem gave an example of what can happen, in Germany, when someone tries to save a wild population of orchids. A woman from Frankfurt discovered that a new roadway was going to demolish a population of indigenous German orchids that grew near her home. The woman, who is a conservationist and an orchid grower, dug up many of the plants and moved them to a nearby location. She was caught moving the plants and fined 10,000 DM. By law, she was required to leave the plants where they would be bulldozed for the roadway. Killing the plants for the road was legal, while moving them to a safe location was punishable by a large fine. Many people have criticized Dr. Braem because he is willing to stand up in front of an audience and point these things out.

"A stupidity, even if it is a legal stupidity, is still a stupidity!" he said. "I am accused of being a criminal, but my answer to that is if it makes me a criminal to save rare orchids, then I am very happy to be a criminal."

At this point the car started to vibrate. Each imperfection in the road threatened to send us airborne as we rocketed down the Autobahn at a speed that can only be described as suicidal. But in all fairness to Dr. Braem's driving, he was simply trying to keep up with the flow of traffic. Sensing my fear, Dr. Braem laughed and tried to reassure me. "What the hell, you crash at 150 kilometers per hour or 220—the result is the same. Only the size of the body pieces are different." I decided to change the topic to food. This did the trick and soon we were coasting to a stop in the parking lot of a roadside restaurant. Once we had taken our seats and ordered lunch, I pulled out a letter from a friend who had attended one of Dr. Braem's orchid lectures in southern California earlier that year. I asked him if he would be interested in hearing the woman's comments.

"Yeah, what the hell, go ahead. Let's hear what the woman has to say!" Dr. Braem laughed.

I smoothed out the letter on the tabletop and began to read the section that I had highlighted:

> . . . and then this large, belligerent German man got up and
> delivered the most astonishing lecture. No one quite knew
> what to make of the guy, but by the time he was finished
> with his talk (and all the side comments that had little if
> anything to do with orchids) he had managed to offend just
> about every religious denomination, gender, family value,
> and dearly held belief of everyone in the room. I guess the
> term "political correctness" hasn't hit Germany yet. No one
> had ever witnessed such an abrasive and entertaining lecture
> on orchids. In any case, once the smoke had cleared from
> the ears and nostrils of those of us seated in the audience, we
> gave him the applause he deserved. He was great. God bless
> him! We want him back!

"Yeah, I remember that group," chuckled Dr. Braem. "Sometimes I get a bit carried away. I thought they were going to string me up with a rope, but after they cooled down it turned out all right. Very nice people."

After a plate of bratwurst and an excellent warm onion-and-potato salad, we returned to the Autobahn, where I had more opportunities to contemplate certain death by mutilation and fire. We had barely gotten up to speed before Dr. Braem began to describe how difficult it was to identify and document new species of orchids. Finding new species in the jungle was not the problem; the most difficult part was getting a plant for which there is not yet a scientific name across international borders. A

CITES permit requires that both the genus and species names of the plant be given, but if the species is unknown to science, the form cannot be filled out completely. This makes it impossible to legally import the plant.

"One day, not too long ago," Dr. Braem recalled, "a gentleman from Wolfsburg walked into my office with a flowering plant of what was no doubt a new species of *Paphiopedilum*. It came from the northeastern corner of the Indonesian island of Sulawesi. The plant had not previously been described. Because it had mistakenly been imported into Germany under the wrong species name, the plant was "illegal." Given my first two encounters with the customs agents, I knew that this orchid was not the sort of thing for me to get caught with. I had the plant on my desk just long enough to photograph it, do the dissection and description, and sketch it. Then I got the damn thing out of my office. I phoned around and found a French orchid journal called *Orchidées—Culture et Protection,* where the editor was delighted to have the honor of publishing the new discovery. Two weeks later, on May 14, 1997, *Paphiopedilum gigantifolium* Braem, Baker & Baker was introduced and I can still hear the howls of protest from my distinguished colleagues in London, Leiden, and elsewhere. A few of them are still screaming that this is further proof that I am an orchid smuggler. Well, I will let you decide these claims for yourself."

Dr. Braem still has the preserved flowers of *Paphiopedilum gigantifolium* in his office, and as everyone knows, these flowers are "illegal." In theory, the authorities could come and take the specimen, fine Dr. Braem, and even throw him in jail because he has a "part" of an illegally imported species of orchid. But how else can a new species be described? If there is no name the plant specimen can't be issued a permit, and without a permit the plant can't be imported legally, unless, of course, you have what Dr. Braem referred to as "the right connections." Since that time, *Paphiopedilum markianum, P. vietnamense, P. tranlienianum,* and *P. hangianum* were all illegally imported because CITES does not have a clause to allow the shipment of new species.

"So, enough about my story," Dr. Braem concluded. "Let's go talk with Popow." Dr. Braem fell silent and we continued down the Autobahn for another half-hour without further discussion. I was numb from listening to Dr. Braem's stories and I wondered how much of what I had heard was true. I would soon have several opportunities to find out, because I was scheduled to meet with CITES officials at their headquarters near Geneva, and with orchid researchers at the Royal Botanic Gardens, Kew, in two weeks. I planned to ask these officials for their side of the conservation story, but over the next few days I was content with what I had heard of Dr. Braem's wealth of anecdotes and tantalizing facts about the inner workings of the orchid world. We finally pulled off the Autobahn and entered the ancient village of Fallersleben. Within minutes we were parked in the courtyard of Bosha Popow's orchid nursery.

Chapter 12

THE ORCHID RAIDS

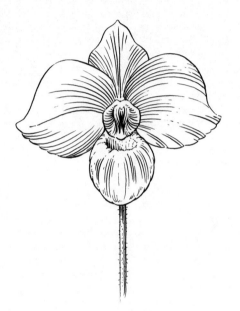

Paphiopedilum delenatii

One crisp winter morning in late February 1988 powdery snowflakes were falling on the old German town of Fallersleben. Light was just beginning to flood the sky, and Bosha Popow was already wandering the aisles of his greenhouse, quietly tending to his orchids. Shortly after dawn, the door to the greenhouse flew open and a group of armed men entered the enclosure. The men wore uniforms and 9-millimeter pistols, and they carried machine guns. Other raiders, in identical combat dress, had already secured the perimeter of the property, and several of them held German shepherd attack dogs on leashes.

"Just like in the days of the Brownshirts," remarked Bosha as he walked me and Dr. Braem around the same greenhouse. Looking at the quiet scene, bathed in moist tropical heat, I found it hard to imagine armed men rushing about the place. The men, as it turned out, were policemen and German customs officers, and from Bosha's description it was clear that they had seriously overdressed for the occasion.

"I was standing here, surrounded by my orchids, and my first thought was that these men were actors who had rushed onto the wrong movie set. They looked like they were storming a hijacked airliner. It was so absurd. But then I went numb when I realized what was happening."

Three or four people from the local conservation authority entered the building along with others from the CITES authority in Frankfurt. Dr. Phillip Cribb, the botanist from the Royal

Botanic Gardens, Kew, had visited the greenhouse in recent weeks after explaining to Bosha how he would very much like to see his fine collection of paphiopedilums. He told Bosha that the visit would be informal and for his personal interest only, but now he was back to identify plants for confiscation.

During the raid Cribb was assisted by his colleague Ed de Vogel from the Botanic Gardens in Leiden. The two men were soon marching up and down the greenhouse aisles, pointing out plants to be confiscated as they called out, "Illegal . . . illegal . . . illegal."

"You should have seen them," Bosha said, shaking his head with disgust. "They could hardly contain themselves. Like a couple of zealots on a horticultural crusade. They were quivering with excitement. They couldn't wait to get their hands on my plants."

"What did you do?" I asked.

"What could I do? I was in shock. I could hardly mutter a coherent word. I ran around like a headless chicken while my plants were being pillaged by these people. My wife had the presence of mind to call Dr. Braem, who left his work and drove five hours through a snowstorm to come help us, and to be a witness to this crude police action that continued through the night and part of the next day."

That night the armed men and their guard dogs patrolled the greenhouse complex. Bosha and Dr. Braem were allowed to water the orchids during the night, but the next day the plants were loaded into unheated trucks and taken away in the snowstorm. The official count of confiscated orchids was 7,658, but many of the pots held four or five plants, which brought the total to approximately 17,000 orchids. The total value of these plants was more than $300,000. According to court documents, many of the orchids were misidentified by Cribb and de Vogel. Bosha never saw the plants again, and it wasn't until much later that he started hearing rumors of where some of his plants ended up.

"Many of them died from neglect in Frankfurt at the botanic garden," he said, "and some died at a garden in Braunschweig for the same reason. Seventeen thousand rare orchids is a very large number to just vanish into thin air, and I have heard that many of them turned up in commercial greenhouses in England, Germany, Holland, California, and elsewhere."

In both the United States and Europe confiscated orchids often go to commercial nurseries designated as rescue centers. The orchids go to these rescue centers because botanical institutions have a reputation for being notoriously bad growers, and for not being able to keep their plants alive. The term "rescue center" suggests some sort of benevolent nonprofit organization run by kind-hearted plant lovers who will tend to the orchids and provide them with a good home. But orchid world insiders know that the confiscated plants are sometimes dispersed as favors to the authorities' friends, regular commercial dealers, and the usual network of "bona fide" botanical institutions. By the time the confiscated orchids arrive at a rescue center they are often dead from neglect, but if the plants are in reasonably good condition or if they can be brought back to health, the rescue center owners have been known to sell, trade, breed, divide, or destroy the plants as they see fit.

An example of how this rescue center redistribution system works took place in Florida in 1989. In February of that year Kerry Richards, owner of the orchid nursery Limerick Inc., received a shipment of Appendix II Chinese paphiopedilums, cymbidiums, and dendrobiums. The shipment had all the paperwork in order, including a commercial invoice, Chinese CITES export permits issued from Canton, and a phytosanitary certificate. Several months later, Mr. Richards decided to enter some of the plants in the Newbury Orchid Show, which is held in the United Kingdom the last week of August. Mr. Richards began the paperwork to get a U.S. CITES re-export permit, but when the show organizers approached U.K. CITES for an import permit they were refused on the grounds that all Chinese paphiopedilums from mainland China were illegal. No known CITES permits had ever been issed by the Chinese authorities, and therefore the assumption was made that the original documents must have been forged or altered.

Mr. Richards contacted the U.S. Department of Fish and Wildlife, asking them to authenticate the original Chinese CITES export permit so that he could send his orchids to the orchid show. By coincidence, a delegation of Chinese forestry officials were visiting the office of the Fish and Wildlife Department. When they were shown the documents, the forestry officials claimed that the CITES office in Canton had no right to issue permits for orchids. Mr. Richards then contacted the CITES secretariat in Geneva for clarification on this point. In response, he was informed that Canton (Guangzhou branch) was, in fact, listed as one of five authorized CITES permit-issuing offices.

In the end, Kerry Richards never received permission to send his plants to the U.K. orchid show, but on Friday, October 2, 1989, he received an unexpected visit from two officers working for the U.S. Department of Fish and Wildlife. One of the officers, Dean Freeman, told Mr. Richards that despite the fact that the Chinese CITES export permits had originally been accepted, it had subsequently been determined that the permits were invalid because they had been altered. For this reason the officers would have to confiscate the plants. Oddly enough, they had no interest in the dendrobiums or cymbidiums, and only the pahpiopedilums were taken. The following Monday all *Paphiopedilum* species were moved onto CITES Appendix 1.

The confiscated plants went to Marie Selby Botanical Gardens in Sarasota, Florida, where some of them were distributed to members, offered for sale, or sent on to other botanical gardens. One lot ended up at the Jardín Lankester in Costa Rica. People at Marie Selby, who prefer to remain anonymous, told me that this was true, and explained that they were not equipped to take such large numbers of plants that needed special attention. They welcomed a few plants for breeding, but they had no interest in providing a haven for plants that were so tainted with political intrigue. Local commercial growers, hobbyists, and others were allowed to buy plants, and although I still find it hard to believe, Kerry Richards could have legally repurchased some of the orchids that had been confiscated from him.

But the story doesn't end there. In response to the orchid confiscation, on November 13, 1989, the *Sarasota Herald-Tribune* ran an inflammatory article about Limerick Inc. smuggling extremely rare and endangered species of orchids from China to Florida. The article quoted the executive director of Marie Selby, Larry Pardue, who explained that the plants were being held under tight security behind locked gates "because it is not uncommon for people to try to recover their property through moonlight raids." This article was distributed to the American Orchid Society membership as part of a drive to raise funds for the orchid rescue center at Marie Selby Gardens. Ironically, Kerry Richards had already donated plants from this shipment to Marie Selby long before the confiscation. The purpose of this donation was to assist in the research and breeding of these desirable orchids. When Kerry pointed this out to them, they claimed that they had never received plants from Limerick Inc., although an American Orchid Society judge, Ethel Goldberg (mother of Bill Goldberg, the professional wrestler), had made such a donation at about the same time. "Yes, I know," Kerry told them, "because I was the one who gave the plants to Ethel and asked her to drop them off for me." Ethel Goldberg later confirmed the details of this story.

Getting back to the Popow raid, not all of his plants disappeared in the snowstorm that cold February day. In fact, some of his very best Chinese paphiopedilums escaped being confiscated because a few weeks before the raid, Gerd Röllke, a former salesman of headache tablets and vice president of the German Orchid Society (Deutsche Orchideen Gesellschaft—known by its acronym DOG), bought approximately 12,000 DM worth of the best paphiopedilums in Popow's nursery. The purchase included *P. micranthum, P. emersonii, P. malipoense,* and *P. armeniacum.* The plants were hand-delivered to Röllke's home in the town of Bielefeld, which is a two- or three-hour drive from Popow's nursery. In 1988 these orchid species, although common in Yunnan Province of China, where they could be bought for around $10 per plant in the flower market of Kunming, were still quite rare in cultivation in Germany and elsewhere. For this reason these plants were expensive and highly sought after by many people in the orchid world.

While Popow's plants were being carted off in a snowstorm, Herr Röllke was tending his newly purchased orchids, which he entered in the DOG annual orchid show held in Marburg the following month. He won the Best of Show with Popow's *Paphiopedilum micranthum,* and received another award for his orchid display, which was made up of the other plants from

Popow's nursery. The show was held in the presence of German CITES authorities, but there was never any question about these plants being "illegal."

Through sheer coincidence, I met Herr Röllke at the 1999 World Orchid Conference in Vancouver, where I had the opportunity to ask him about his award-winning Chinese paphiopedilums that he bought from Popow just prior to the raid in 1988. Herr Röllke told me he had won so many prestigious awards over the years that he could no longer keep track of each one. I pressed the issue and asked him to explain at precisely what point the orchids had become legal. I wanted to know why, in his role as vice president of the German Orchid Society, he had not immediately turned in the plants to the authorities after the raid on Popow's nursery. In response, he blurted out that he couldn't remember the plants.

Following the raid on his orchid nursery, Bosha Popow was charged with smuggling orchids. The prosecution asked for a two-year prison sentence and a 750,000 DM fine, and this sent out a clear message that the authorities wanted to ruin Popow financially and close his nursery. The court case ran from 1988 until 1992. In the end he was not convicted of any crime, but he paid a 10,000 DM fine with no admission of guilt. Despite the outcome of the case and the misidentification of hundreds of plants, he never had his orchids returned, nor did he receive compensation for them.

The raid on Popow's orchid nursery was not unique. Similar raids have been carried out at orchid nurseries in Belgium, France, Holland, England, Canada, the United States, and possibly elsewhere.

"It would be silly for me to claim that out of my collection there were no wild-collected plants," said Bosha. "And I won't tell you that there are no orchid collectors, because they exist. But if you walk into certain well-known botanic gardens in the world you will also find wild-collected orchids in those institutions. The only difference between my plants and their plants is that the people who helped move all paphiopedilums, phragmipediums, and some other exotic orchids onto CITES Appendix I—the most endangered list—they made sure, through sleight of hand, that their wild-collected plants were suddenly 'legal,' while everyone else's plants were 'illegal.' Where do you think they got their wild orchids from? From the same set of private collectors that everyone used until the rules were changed in 1989. Large botanical institutions will deny this, but they still have privileged access to rare wild-collected orchids. The rest of us are harassed and regulated to death by the authorities. I am an orchid grower. My work has not changed, it is the rules that changed and now my work is suddenly against the law."

Popow disputed the claim that the present rate of trade in wild-collected orchids has any significant effect on native orchid populations. Most of the "smuggling," he felt, is done by orchid hobbyists on vacation. They bring back a few plants for their collection and maybe a plant or two for sale.

There are wealthy orchid people around the world who will pay large sums for rare plants. I have met many in Tokyo, Hong Kong, Zurich, London, Frankfurt, Chicago, Los Angeles, and Sydney. They have shown me their collections, most of which fit on a windowsill, or, in rare cases, in a greenhouse the size of a small bedroom. There are not many of these affluent growers, but they exist. A wild-collected sanderianum sells for about $600 per growth, which means that for a mature plant with two, three, or four growths, a decent amount of money is involved. But as anyone in the business will tell you, it is not possible to sell one hundred mature sanderianum per year at these prices. The market is very limited. The yearly sales figures for wild-collected species are insignificant. Bosha gave me some approximate trade figures for Germany, based on his wide knowledge of the international orchid trade.

"In the German population of 86 million people, a maximum of fifteen rothschildianums and fifteen sanderianums can be sold each year, and most of those plants go into breeding programs. These numbers are not going to affect any native plant population. In addition to this, demand for wild plants is rapidly declining, because more and more excellent specimens are becoming available from artificially propagated plants produced in commercial nurseries.

"You can't go on the market with 500 *Paphiopedilum stonei*," Bosha explained, "and expect to sell them at a good price. That is nonsense. Supply and demand controls the market price. *Paphiopedilum hookerae* used to go for $3,000 in the late 1970s. Now you can get good plants for around $50 or less and the price will only go down. Give the nursery business another ten years and all of the paphiopedilums and other exotic orchids in cultivation will be raised in commercial nurseries from seed."

Overland orchid-smuggling routes come and go, but anyone in the plant business in Europe knows which international airports to fly to with hand-carried plants. These channels are well established. I have watched how it works; the technique is simple and effective. In eastern Europe there are innumerable border crossings from the Czech Republic and Poland because these two countries have not joined CITES. If you need a few orchids you have them mailed to either one of these countries. Once they arrive, you just drive there, put the plants in the car, and go home. The very best market for orchids is in Japan; although I am by no means an expert in these matters, I know three different ways to get plants to Japan. Taiwan is a favorite place to "launder" plants because they never signed the CITES convention. They are prevented from doing so because the United Nations does not recognize them as a country. As a result, Taiwan has accumulated some of the best orchid breeding stock in the world. For people in a hurry, postal courier services are used to send small numbers of select orchids worldwide. Orchids are generally not shipped when they are in flower, so with nearly 25,000 species and 100,000 hybrids to choose from, it is also very easy to use the official CITES permits and simply substitute one orchid name for another.

The day I visited Popow's nursery, he had invited several other orchid hobbyists to join us in the afternoon for coffee and cake. We sat in his office, where I listened to their stories for two hours. These men did not want their names mentioned, but they were willing to tell me about how they had been treated by "the orchid police." A kindly, middle-aged ophthalmologist explained how his office was raided during normal business hours by armed men. "You can imagine what a reassuring effect this had on my patients in the waiting room," he said. "The idiots went through the file drawers of my surgery looking for records of illegal orchid purchases. They found nothing because there was nothing to find. I was lucky because they could have taken the file cabinets with my medical billing records."

A second man, a schoolteacher, was taken out of his classroom by armed officials. He asked the men not to handcuff him in front of the children, and in the end the officials agreed that it would be bad form to do so. They drove the teacher to his house, where they confiscated seven orchids. No charges were brought against the man, but the plants were never returned.

Back at school, the teacher had a difficult time convincing his students and the school administration that the incident had been about his modest collection of orchids.

After cake and coffee at Popow's nursery, Dr. Braem and I continued our drive through northern Germany and then into Belgium and the Netherlands. At each orchid nursery I heard similar tales of harassment, fines, and confiscation of orchids. The orchid growers felt that these police actions were part of an effort to bring the international orchid trade to a grinding halt.

The idea of monitoring the international trade in orchids is a good one, but as Bruce Weissgold, who is an intelligence specialist with the U.S. Fish and Wildlife Service, points out, "No one has compiled an accurate inventory of the world's orchid stock." Without hard data on the locations and population numbers of specific orchid species in the wild, it is not possible to determine how much collecting will adversely affect the species. Educated guesses are no substitute for hard data, and the danger of using soft data is that it paves the way for policy decisions that are based on prejudice and self-interest.

Looking at CITES worldwide trade data (compiled by the World Conservation Monitoring Centre in Cambridge, United Kingdom) for the years 1987 through 1994, I found the import/export figures for artificially propagated *Paphiopedilum sanderianum*, the CITES Appendix I slipper orchid that I have seen growing by the untold thousands on Fire Mountain in Sarawak. In 1988 the total world trade was around 1,500 plants; in 1987 it was approximately 500 plants, with the remaining years ranging from a dozen plants in 1989 to a couple of hundred plants in 1992. The average came to a little more than 300 plants per year. No one keeps written records on the number of smuggled plants, but by following the dubious practice (of Traffic International and other monitoring organizations) of linking legal and illegal trade, let us assume that the illegal trade represents a small fraction of the legal trade. An educated guess would put the number of wild-collected sanderianum plants at several dozen per year; with a figure like this it would be difficult if not impossible to come up with a convincing argument that illegal trade has any effect whatsoever on the wild populations of *Paphiopedilum sanderianum*. And this is the orchid that the experts hold up as a flagship species—a prime example of a species facing imminent extinction because of illegal collection and trade.

Despite the lack of data on wild populations of exotic orchids, CITES continues to try to strongly discourage or halt the trade in orchid species, and to bog down the trade in nursery-grown orchid hybrids with a cumbersome permit system. The principal means used, as in Popow's case, are highly publicized police raids and plant confiscations. It appears the rationale behind this effort is that with sufficient pressure on commercial growers, the collectors will have difficulty selling wild-collected plants, heightened public awareness will cause the market to dry up, and the plants will be able to live happily ever after in their natural environment.

Of the hundreds of well-informed growers, hobbyists, and botanists that I have spoken with over the years, not one of them goes along with this piecemeal approach to orchid conservation. They claim that twenty years of trade restrictions and ten years of orchid nursery raids have made no significant contribution to orchid conservation or research. To the contrary, as a direct result of trade restrictions, botanists find it difficult if not impossible to obtain plant specimens for scientific research, and in the field of orchid conservation, the restrictions have discouraged or prevented salvage operations.

A few months after I finished driving from greenhouse to greenhouse with Dr. Braem, I met Dr. John H. Beaman, who was working at the University of Malaysia as director of the Institute of Biodiversity and Environmental Conservation. He was also working on a book about the flora of Mount Kinabalu, a mountain located in the East Malaysian state of Sabah, on the island of Borneo. I have spent weeks exploring the slopes of Mount Kinabalu and the nearby mountains on foot, and this is where you will find many rare and exotic plants such as the slipper orchid *Paphiopedilum rothschildianum,* and several spectacular species of giant pitcher plants, especially *Nepenthes rajah* and *N. edwardsiana.* Dr. Beaman and I have common friends who work as botanists in Borneo and we have all visited many of the same remote areas. Dr. Beaman is the recipient of a prestigious MacArthur Grant and has enjoyed a long and distinguished career as a field botanist and an educator. When I asked him for his candid opinion on CITES, he told me that the regulations, as they are being implemented, "are an unfortunate and unnecessary hindrance to commercial growers, researchers, and hobbyists. All the treaty has done," he said, "is harass the honest people. The crooks will always find a way to move the plants. There is nothing CITES can do to control demand and they are merely driving prices up with their total ban on trade in desirable species."

Commercial growers shy away from CITES because they have found that their sales of artificially propagated species and nursery-grown hybrids are being regulated by a permit system that has nothing to do with the conservation of wild plants. But the greatest irony of all, I discovered, is that the press coverage of orchid smuggling and the listing of certain plants as endangered species have greatly increased the demand for rare orchids. This in turn has driven up prices and led to an even bigger market for the plants. Knowledgeable botanists and commercial growers believe that the only way to deal with collecting and trade threats for most plant species (not just orchids) is to make artificially propagated plants affordable and readily available, especially near where they grow in the wild.

Popow told me that by the time his case was thrown out of court his business was doing better than before the raid. Orchid people now flocked to his nursery because of the publicity, and the increased demand allowed him to raise his prices for both species and hybrids. Now when customers attempt to bargain over the price of any plant, Popow jokingly informs them the plant is "illegal," so they must pay a higher price.

The final stop on our orchid nursery tour was Orchideeën Wubben, a Dutch nursery just north of Utrecht. When we arrived there was no one in the nursery, so we walked over to a nearby house where we found Koos Wubben setting out lunch in anticipation of our arrival. Our host is highly regarded in the European orchid world for growing fine plants, but he has also attained folk hero status for getting caught at Amsterdam's Schiphol Airport with Costa Rican orchids taped to his body.

"Oh yes!" Koos laughed. "They caught me with the orchids. No doubt about it. When they found the plants I just shrugged my shoulders, and they took me into custody."

I tried to imagine myself standing in a customs inspection room as humorless men in crisp uniforms photographed me with my trousers around my ankles and dozens of orchids fastened to my legs with duct tape. It would be excruciatingly difficult, if not impossible, for any normal person to maintain a straight face in such a situation.

As we were eating lunch, Koos explained why he had made the decision to import the orchids in such an unconventional manner. "I go to Costa Rica every year to buy orchids and when I am there I have limited time. It can take weeks to obtain the CITES export permits from Costa Rica, and no commercial grower can afford to waste that kind of time buying plants. The CITES import permit for the Netherlands can take as long as ten weeks to be issued. The people here tell me to fill out the forms before I go to Costa Rica, but these trips are for finding new plants, so I don't know exactly what I will be bringing back until after I get there. What I don't like about exporting orchids from Costa Rica is the bureaucracy."

Koos Wubben described a certain unpaid "botanical expert" whose job it is to verify the identity of each orchid in the shipment for the CITES officials. To get this verification, you are expected to pay a "gratuity," and of course the larger the shipment and the more urgently you need to get the verification, the higher the gratuity. This is also a big problem in Brazil, and in other countries as well.

"I got fed up with paying bribes," Koos explained. "Why should I pay to obtain CITES documents for legal, nursery-grown plants? I lost my temper and so I taped the plants to my body and went to the airport. It was an idiotic thing to do. Realizing that I had left the country without paying anything, the 'botanical expert' got suspicious. The customs authorities in Amsterdam were alerted and that is how I was caught."

Koos admitted that he was guilty of transporting ninety young orchid seedlings without proper documentation, but he pointed out that they were nursery-grown and that the plants certainly were not worth the $2,000 each that the local newspaper had claimed. The real problem for commercial growers like Koos Wubben is the time-consuming paperwork and the corrupt officials who prey on every botanist, orchid hobbyist, and grower that comes their way. The experience was enough to make him consider giving up on buying orchids in Costa Rica. The regulations, as implemented, encourage most other people to simply forgo the proper procedures and just buy the plants and hand-carry or ship them home any way possible.

After lunch and a tour of Orchideeën Wubben, Dr. Braem took me to the train station in Utrecht. From there I returned to Paris, where I spent a leisurely time visiting friends and typing up my notes as I digested what I had been told by the European orchid growers.

During my stay in Paris I decided to visit the orchid nursery of Marcel Lecoufle in the nearby town of Boissy-Saint-Léger. Marcel is now in his eighties, and the daily operations of the nursery are run by his daughter Geneviève and granddaughter Isabelle. Together, they manage Marcel Lecoufle Orchidées, one of the oldest and most distinguished orchid-breeding facilities in the world. The nursery is open to the public. I wanted to see their collection of *Paphiopedilum delenatii,* for which they are famous. In 1913 a French military officer brought a live specimen from Tonkin (Vietnam) to Paris. It was grown by Mr. Delénat, the head gardener at the palace of Saint-Germain-en-Laye, and later at the gardens of Saint-Cloud. Around 1925, divisions of this plant were given to the greenhouses at the Museum of Natural History in Paris; and eventually one of the plants was sent to the Lecoufle nursery at Boissy-Saint-Léger. Initially, the Lecoufle family propagated *Paphiopedilum delenatii* by sowing seeds on the compost of the mother plant, but later they greatly increased production through the revolutionary use of in vitro techniques which they developed. In this manner, the Lecoufle nursery managed to keep delenatii in cultivation and available to scientists and growers for more than half a century. It was thought to be extinct in the wild, and only in 1993 when the plant was rediscovered in Vietnam did wild-collected plants become widely available on the international market. This, by the way, is a prime example of CITES not being able to manage trade by controlling the export and import of rare plant species.

Probably the most important but least-known contribution of the Lecoufle family to the orchid world was the introduction of tissue culture propagation of orchids on a commercial scale. The nursery has also been a world leader in hybridizing odontoglossums, paphiopedilums, brassocattleyas, miltonias, phalaenopsis, and semi-alba yellow cattleyas. Just before World War I they acquired a number of *Phalaenopsis* species from Indonesia, including *P. amabilis, P. stuartiana, P. rimestadiana,* and *P. schilleriana.* This shipment provided the original breeding stock for the spectacular range of large white *Phalaenopsis* hybrids that are so popular today. The Lecoufle family has played a central role in orchid research, hybridizing, and species conservation for more than one hundred years, which makes what happened to them in 1991 all the more puzzling.

While I was being shown through the nursery by Isabelle, I casually asked her if they had ever had any difficulties with customs inspectors. Isabelle looked at me for a long moment, smiled, and then said, "If you would like to hear the story, I am sure my grandfather will tell it to you." We returned to the nursery office, where Marcel described their ordeal.

"Concerning our problems," he began, "here are the main details. At Les Floralies de Nantes [a major flower exhibit held once every five years in the city of Nantes], in May 1989, Isabelle purchased a group of *Paphiopedilum* species from an exhibitor. His name was Mr. Kabukiran and he was an orchid grower from the Philippines. These plants were for sale. We bought them at the end of the show for a good price because Mr. Kabukiran was going to throw them away because of the paperwork involved in taking them back to the Philippines. Other orchid growers bought the same plants from him, and the next year these orchids were put on CITES Appendix I—the endangered list. The purchase was done correctly with official invoices, but we had not thought about or requested any CITES permit from Mr. Kabukiran. He brought the plants through French customs, customs inspectors were present at Les Floralies, and so we assumed they entered the country legally."

Two years later Marcel Lecoufle received a visit from a young lady who spoke English and told him that she was a student at the Museum of Natural History in Paris. She did not give her name to Monsieur Lecoufle, but she was very interested in looking at his collection of paphiopedilums. When they were standing in front of the group of orchids that Isabelle had bought from Mr. Kabukiran, the woman asked Marcel where the plants had come from. He didn't know, but he told her that she should ask his daughter Geneviève or his granddaughter Isabelle because they were the ones who managed the nursery. They were gone for the day, so Marcel couldn't answer the lady's question. This woman also visited other commercial and amateur growers in the area. It wasn't long before Marcel discovered her true identity. Her name was Mrs. Blaise DuPuy and she was the person who reported the Lecoufle nursery to the French customs office.

Blaise DuPuy was then the wife of David DuPuy, who, at the time of the raid on the Lecoufle nursery, worked at Kew, where he co-authored the book *The Genus Cymbidium* with his friend and colleague Phillip Cribb.

Marcel continued with his story. "The French customs inspectors came to our nursery and seized about four hundred of our plants. The confiscated orchids were sent to the Conservatoire et Jardins Botaniques in Nancy, where many of them have died in the following years. We hear rumors that some of these plants were sold or exchanged, but it is not possible to know for sure. It would take too long to give you all the complications and tribulations we have had with this affair."

"The documents for our court case are one foot thick," Isabelle said as she opened a file drawer to show me the papers. "Look at this newspaper article," she said, handing me a cutting from the *Evening Post,* a newspaper published in New Zealand. The customs agents took only 400 plants from the Lecoufle nursery, but by the time the case appeared in the newspaper on the other side of the world the number of plants had grown to 2,000, including twenty-two threatened species and three extinct species.

"The customs officers told us that if we should pay 90,000 francs and give up the plants, the matter would be dropped. But we refused to pay," said Marcel. "By 1993 they wanted 419,000 francs, also without returning our plants. We argued that many people and botanic gardens bought the same plants from Mr. Kabukiran, but only we were denounced. We could have mentioned all the other growers that had the same plants, but we are part of the orchid-growing community and it is not for us to behave in this way. We protested that if a CITES permit was necessary to import the plants, it should have been given by the customs services of Nantes at the point of entry. Mr. Kabukiran has never been pursued, but in orchid publications around the world in New Zealand, England, Canada, and the United States, I am called a smuggler of orchids! Ridiculous! We are producers of orchids, not smugglers. We make 150,000 new orchid plants each year."

Isabelle described a phone call her mother, Geneviève, had made to the World Wildlife Fund in Paris on January 5, 1995. Geneviève wanted to talk to the president, Mr. J. B. Dumont, to discuss the details of their case, but a secretary refused to let her speak with him. Instead, the woman just told her bluntly, "We don't want to talk! We just want the money and to make an example of you!"

Geneviève and Isabelle went to court at Creteil on February 22, 1995. The French customs director was asking for a 1,200,000 franc fine, with the World Wildlife Fund demanding an additional 60,000 francs. Shocked by these amounts, Isabelle pointed out that the fine for possession of 500 grams of heroin and 30 kilograms of hashish would only come to 300,000 francs. At the trial the judge refused the World Wildlife Fund's request for 60,000 francs, but because of the complexity of the case and the late hour, deliberations were postponed until a later date. On May 10, 1995, the Lecoufle family agreed to pay a fine of 60,000 francs without getting their plants returned. The total purchase price for the plants six years earlier had come to only 26,875 francs.

"Well, thank you for showing me your beautiful collection of *Paphiopedilum delenatii*," I joked as I got ready to leave. Isabelle handed me a large envelope filled with photocopied letters and court papers. Marcel shook my hand, and as I walked down the hill toward the train station I realized that I was finally ready to pay a visit to the Royal Botanic Gardens, Kew.

Chapter 13

A VISIT
TO KEW GARDENS

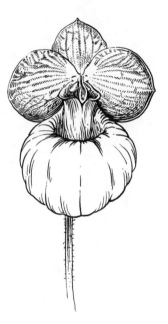

Paphiopedilum micranthum

From Piccadilly Circus I took the London Underground to the Royal Botanic Gardens, Kew, in the Greater London borough of Richmond. I had come to this world-renowned botanical institution to meet Dr. Phillip Cribb, the curator of the Orchid Herbarium. After I signed in at the front door, a security guard made a phone call to Dr. Cribb, who came down to the lobby to pick me up and show me around his domain. We set off on foot and within minutes the musty smell of the place with its dark, wood-paneled corridors, oak display cases, wax-scented floors, towering bookcases of leather-bound volumes, framed portraits, and historical prints had me in a trance. I thought of the great botanists and administrators who had distinguished themselves at Kew, like Sir Joseph Banks, Sir William Hooker and his intrepid plant-collecting son Joseph Dalton Hooker, and William T. Thiselton-Dyer. The bottles of pickled specimens, the hush of the library, and the sight of wizened researchers hunched over their herbarium sheets with magnifying glasses and microscopes perfectly captured the history, tradition, and magic of the place.

Despite all that I had been told about Dr. Cribb, I took an immediate liking to him. There was something refreshing and uncomplicated about the man that I found very reassuring. Phillip Cribb is extremely handsome and well groomed. His tousled hair and boyish good looks give an impression of youthful innocence, and his soft-spoken and earnest way of talking immediately set me at ease. He has long, delicate fingers and the meticulously clipped and scrubbed fingernails of a surgeon. He is articulate, charming, and utterly convincing when he starts talking about his passion in life, which is orchids. Dr. Cribb exuded a surprisingly warm and cordial presence.

Dr. Cribb is the co-editor of the *Handbook of Orchid Nomenclature and Registration* and the author of the very beautifully illustrated book *The Genus Paphiopedilum*, now in its second edition. Along with Helmut Bechtel and Edmund Launert, he also wrote the *Manual of Cultivated Orchid Species*. His writing has also appeared in the British gardening publication *The Plantsman*. Dr. Cribb is a member of the Royal Horticultural Society and was recently appointed chairman of the Orchid Specialist Group of the IUCN World Conservation Union. He is probably the most politically powerful individual in the orchid world today. I asked Dr. Cribb how he became involved with orchids.

"Well, when I was a boy, my grandfather got me interested in collecting butterflies and other insects. I guess that's where it all started. He instilled in me a love of nature and a love of wild things. Once I began my work at Kew I discovered the world of orchids, and over the years I have made them my specialty. Conservation of plant species is a guiding principle here at Kew and I want to make sure that my children will be able to enjoy the plants that I knew as a child."

After introducing me to the head librarian, Dr. Cribb walked me over to an adjoining brick building. We entered a back door and followed a rabbit warren of stairs and passageways to the office of Mr. Noel McGough, who is the conservation officer at Kew. With his staff he carries out the CITES Scientific Authority for Plants in the United Kingdom. Noel is in charge of licensing nurseries, evaluating the legitimacy of artificial propagation programs, correcting species names, monitoring trade, issuing import permits, and making judgment calls on imported plant shipments. He has the power to order plant inspections at all ports of entry, and he serves on the advisory board of the Kew Herbarium. As I shook hands with Noel I couldn't help noticing a large color portrait of Henry Azadehdel pinned to his bulletin board like some sort of trophy.

Once the formalities were completed, Dr. Cribb escorted Noel and me to a small room just off the stairway. He closed the door and the three of us sat around a large table in what looked like a staff meeting room. Given the considerable power and reputations of these two men and the fact that Kew is the principal advisor to the CITES Secretariat in Geneva, I looked forward to our talk.

I had a long list of topics that I wanted to discuss regarding the orchid trade, but before I could ask my first question Dr. Cribb leaned across the table and asked me about my point of view on orchid conservation and CITES regulations. I told him I had collected a great deal of information that I wanted to discuss with him, and explained that the reason I had come to Kew was to get their point of view. They were the expert authorities on all aspects of the orchid trade, and I made it clear that I had come to ask questions, to listen, and to learn.

I asked Dr. Cribb how many species of orchids had been saved from extinction by regulating trade, and which species of orchids had become extinct because of overcollecting. He didn't have any numbers or names for me, and suggested that I speak with Ger van Vliet, the plants officer at the CITES headquarters in Geneva. (Dr. van Vliet responded to these questions a few weeks later with a rather haughty "How would I know?") At about this point in the conversation I noticed that Noel was shifting uncomfortably in his chair.

I was curious to know why so many of the late twentieth-century plant conservation laws seemed to be designed to combat nineteenth-century mass collecting practices that were no longer used. The conversation wandered and turned to trivia for a short while. Then we briefly discussed the idea of orchid salvage operations in parts of Malaysia that were going to be logged. Dr. Cribb told me that such orchid salvage would not work, because there was no way to prevent the collectors from taking orchids from the adjoining areas as well.

"With the hundreds of thousands of orchids to collect within the logging concession, who would have the time or interest to go into other areas?" I asked. "And what about the orchids at risk within the logging area?" I was surprised by Dr. Cribb's reply.

"I don't know who you represent, or what sort of book you are writing, but I don't want to have anything to do with it."

What is going on here? I thought to myself.

I had exchanged letters, faxes, and e-mail with Dr. Cribb over the previous months. In one fax he told me how he had enjoyed reading my Borneo book, *Stranger in the Forest,* and that he would be happy to meet with me during my visit. I had even given him a general idea of what I wanted to discuss. He encouraged me to come visit, and a secretary at the Royal Botanic Gardens office had booked me a room at a local guest house for a week so that I would have plenty of time to look through the library and herbarium and to talk to Dr. Cribb and other botanists about orchid trade and conservation.

During our brief conversation, which lasted no longer than ten minutes, Noel sat at the table without saying more than a few words. Considering the immense power that these two men had over the worldwide plant trade, I was dumbfounded by their reluctance to talk openly about their work.

I found it odd that when interviewing "orchid smugglers" like Dr. Braem, Bosha Popow, Harto Kolopaking (whom I interviewed by mail while he was in federal prison in Lompoc, California), Marcel Lecoufle, and Henry Azadehdel, I could hardly get them to shut up. Without exception, they had all been eager to divulge the contents of their file drawers, show me personal letters and court documents, and tell me what had happened to them. But now that I was with two of the most powerful advocates for orchid trade controls in the United Kingdom and the rest of the world, I found it was next to impossible to get any information from them.

Dr. Cribb broke the awkward silence by asking me what more he could do to "help" me. Would I like to look at some back issues of the *Gardener's Chronicle* to glean ideas for my book?

I told him that I would rather discuss orchid conservation and find out more about his connection with the orchid collector Henry Azadehdel. Noel finally excused himself in order to get back to work. He invited me to come visit with him the following day, and we set a time. Then Dr. Cribb and I retraced our steps through the labyrinth of stairways and returned to his office in the adjoining building.

"What I am trying to do is bring a higher level of discourse to the orchid world," Dr. Cribb explained, as he took his seat at his desk.

"That sounds like an excellent idea," I said. "But what can you tell me about Henry Azadehdel and his connection to Kew prior to his arrest? Henry has told me that he collected rare species of paphiopedilums for you. He claims that plants were shipped directly to you from Hong Kong, Indonesia, and elsewhere, and that Kew arranged CITES import permits for some of the plants. Is this true?"

"Absolute rubbish!" he laughed.

Dr. Cribb wasn't particularly keen to talk about Henry. He denied any official or unofficial contact with him and then dismissed Henry as "a rather pathetic orchid thief, an enthusiastic amateur who came snooping around Kew to look for habitat information on rare orchids." Dr. Cribb also denied having ever asked for or received any wild-collected orchids, either live or dead, from Henry. "As you know, I deal exclusively with pickled or dried orchid specimens," he explained curtly.

I also asked him about Dr. Guido Braem's taxonomic work with orchids. But rather than responding to my question immediately, Dr. Cribb paused for a long moment as if he was having trouble remembering anyone by that name. "Oh yes, the German chap," he finally said. "Part of the German orchid mafia, isn't he? I believe I was on his Ph.D. examination panel. As I recall, Braem's thesis was bullshit. Something about oncidiums in the Caribbean."

This comment did not come as a complete surprise, because it is a well-known fact in the orchid world that Dr. Cribb and Dr. Braem are not on good terms. In 1985 Dr. Braem legitimately renamed *Paphiopedilum devogelii* (an undescribed species that had been informally attributed to Cribb's close friend Ed de Vogel) as *Paphiopedilum supardii* (after the Indonesian man who collected the type specimen). A similar specimen of the plant had been sitting in a herbarium cabinet at Kew for years, but no one had taken the time to complete the scientific description and legally name the plant after de Vogel. As a result, Dr. Braem's description and new name were published first. When Dr. Cribb protested, Dr. Braem defended himself by telling his colleagues: "How am I supposed to know what dead plants Dr. Cribb keeps in his herbarium drawers?" Bad blood has existed between the two men ever since.

On October 2, 1987, Dr. Cribb returned the favor by writing a letter to Dr. Jelden at German CITES. In the letter he claimed that Dr. Braem, Henry Azadehdel, and Bosha Popow were part of an international network of orchid smugglers. He then offered his services to help stop their activities and put them out of business. At the conclusion of his letter he suggested that if just one orchid smuggler could be sent to jail, then the others would fall into line and this would help bring the illegal orchid trade to an end. Two months later Henry Azadehdel was arrested and his orchid collection was confiscated. The following February Popow's nursery was raided. In both cases Dr. Cribb took part in the raids, and in both cases Dr. Braem was hired as an expert for the defense.

As these and other details were swirling through my mind I still couldn't help but wonder how such a mild-mannered and distinguished-looking botanist as Dr. Cribb could get caught up in such activities. In addition to looking distinguished, he enjoys a wide following and a considerable reputation in the orchid world. In the words of one of his friends and colleagues, "Without a doubt, Phil has been one of the most prolific authors and contibutors in the history of orchid literature. He has either authored or co-authored innumerable monographs and floras [geographical treatments]. He is a taxonomic expert on African orchids and the leading authority on the genus *Polystachya*. He is also the current expert on the genus *Cypripedium*, especially the Asian species, and of course has a reputation for *Paphiopedilum*, although he is not active in naming new species in that genus. Phil has traveled extensively throughout the world looking at orchids in the wild, and under his stewardship the Orchid Herbarium at Kew has attained worldwide status as a special place in the orchid world. He also has special concerns for orchid conservation."

My remaining conversation with Dr. Cribb was brief. I never had an opportunity to ask him about his connection to Blaise DuPuy and the raid on the Lecoufle nursery because he suddenly excused himself. He said he was "terribly sorry" but he had to "dash off" for a meeting with the keeper of the herbarium. Dr. Cribb was kind enough to authorize my temporary visitor's card, which allowed me access to the library and herbarium, but within minutes we were shaking hands and he was striding down the hallway. The sound of his hurried footsteps soon blended with the gentle murmur of activity that fills the hallowed corridors of Kew. I continued to visit Kew for the rest of the week, but apart from a brief encounter with Dr. Cribb in the Orchid Herbarium the following day and once for lunch at a pub down the road, I never saw him again during my visit.

Over the following years, however, I continued to correspond with Dr. Cribb, asking about persistent rumors and documents and letters that seemed to confirm that Henry had collected orchids for Kew. I especially wanted to know about the falling-out between these two men. Despite my assiduous efforts to get Dr. Cribb's version of events, I continued to receive brief but courteous and charming replies of little substance. The last time I saw Dr. Cribb was in January of 1999 at the World Orchid Conference in Vancouver. During the conference he presided over the IUCN Orchid Specialty Group as its new chairman. He also delivered a very stimulating lecture on orchid conservation, titled "Gone Is Forever: An Overview of Orchids in the Wild—Present Status and Threats." At the opening reception I asked him, for the last time, about Henry Azadehdel and his connection to Kew. Dr. Cribb replied sharply, "Henry never had . . . and never will have ANYTHING to do with Kew."

The morning after my initial meeting with Dr. Cribb, I visited Noel McGough in his office. This time he was much more relaxed and talkative. He was candid enough to tell me that the data on endangered species of orchids "was really just hit or miss." He was equally forthright in his description of the way CITES functions. "With 132 member countries it is the old problem of controlling the people who want to do the controlling. CITES wrecked the legitimate worldwide seed trade business, and it is unfortunate that the organization gets bogged down in so much petty political infighting."

Noel also provided me with the name of Crawford Allan, the enforcement officer at TRAFFIC International, the bird-dog conservation group that watches and analyzes the worldwide trade in flora and fauna species. CITES uses statistics and reports from TRAFFIC to develop resolutions that control the orchid trade. On the phone, Mr. Allan told me that the figures for smuggled orchids are just guesswork. The numbers are not based on hard fact, but rather on an arbitrary percentage of the total number of orchids traded legally.

Over at the Micropropagation Unit, Margaret Ramsey talked about her efforts to help conserve endangered British orchids such as *Cypripedium calceolus* (subspecies *calceolus*). According to orchid conservation lore, in the 1930s this species had been reduced to one known plant in the United Kingdom because of gardeners' digging up live plants and botanical institutions' overcollecting for their herbarium specimens. "Several of our most distinguished institutions"—which she asked me not to mention by name—"had as many as forty herbarium sheets of the same species, collected from the same locality in consecutive years, and sometimes by the same collector! Absolutely no excuse for this sort of work on scientific grounds." In the most extreme case Margaret could remember, an overzealous institutional collector had taken seventeen plants from a total population of eighteen, all for herbarium specimens.

This sort of obsessive collecting, pressing, and drying of plants made me think about phyto-necrophilia, which is the abnormal fascination with or love of dead plant material. The expression "phyto-necrophiliac" is sometimes used among botanists to describe sedentary scholars who detest fieldwork and confine their taxonomic studies to dead plants in the herbarium. These are the sort of researchers who might relish the prospect of a rainy afternoon spent rehydrating dried flower petals or untangling the desiccated roots and leaves of dead plants under a dissecting microscope. Despite the obvious importance of this sort of work, it can lead to a sort of horticultural rapture that I am entirely unfamiliar with.

The Royal Botanic Gardens, Kew, are situated along the east bank of the River Thames. The gardens are spread over 330 acres, and during my visit I spent an entire day wandering from one splendid greenhouse and pavilion to the next, along meandering pathways that led through native woodlands to rose gardens, past pools with giant waterlilies, into herbal gardens, scented gardens, and even a bee garden. At unexpected moments broad lanes opened to reveal distant views of the towering Pagoda or the magnificent Palm House, which dates from 1848.

This immense structure of light and form is an architectural dream of lacy ironwork and glass that looks translucent and delicate as a gigantic, curvilinear insect wing. Enormous trees shaded park benches where elderly people and nannies with their baby strollers sat down for a rest and gazed at expanses of undulating lawn. I discovered one area devoted entirely to grasses and another to carnivorous plants. According to the visitor's brochure, there are 40,000 different types of plants in the collection. No visit to the gardens would be complete without afternoon tea, and so I stopped at the Orangery for a pot of Earl Grey accompanied by scones, Devonshire clotted cream, and rasberry jam before continuing my walk.

That afternoon I discovered the Sir Joseph Banks Center for Economic Botany, which is a treasure-house of plants used for medicine, food, magic, fabric dyes, clothing, shelter, and much more. In the bamboo garden I met a sympathetic groundskeeper who took me into the Cycad House (closed to the public) to show me examples of these ancient palmlike plants, which have remained little changed since dinosaurs nibbled their stiff leaves.

The groundskeeper gave me her views on plant collecting. "In the sixteenth century Britain had maybe 200 plants in cultivation, but by the nineteenth century we had around 18,000 in cultivation. Where did these flowers, shrubs, and trees come from?" she asked. "The empire builders ransacked them from the Amazon, Siberia, Australia, China, India, Turkey, South Africa, and everywhere else they could get their hands on them. Some of these new plants could not survive the climate in Britain, and that is why King George III built Kew. He hired Sir Joseph Banks, the botanist on Captain Cook's ship the HMS *Endeavour,* to manage the gardens. Kew botanists on the HMS *Providence* took breadfruit from Polynesia to be grown as cheap slave food in the West Indies, and Sir Joseph sent botanists on every British ship that he could for the purpose of bringing back plants of economic importance. Kew is a very learned botanical institution, but don't forget that we are standing in the middle of the largest collection of horticultural loot on earth."

Banks, who initiated what many have called Kew's international plant-plundering program, got his start in this sort of business by smuggling merino sheep from Spain to Portugal. From Portugal the sheep were transported to England, where the animals grazed at Kew for a while until a select few went to Sydney, Australia, where the breed ignited the Australian wool boom. Sir Joseph was man of wide interests and appetites. In 1766, at the age of twenty-four, he visited Newfoundland aboard a naval vessel and later returned to England with a collection of insects, rocks, and dead birds, with an Indian scalp thrown in for good measure. In 1769 he was in Tahiti with Cook to observe the transit of the planet Venus, and while awaiting this event (the observation of which would facilitate celestial navigation everywhere on earth), he attended a local funeral wearing nothing but a gritty coating of water and charcoal. Following these formative experiences, Banks returned to England, where he transformed Kew into a center for the global transfer of plants.

Even a perfunctory knowledge of how the seeds and stem cuttings from the rubber tree (*Hevea brasiliensis*) were taken illegally from Brazil to Southeast Asia, via Kew, reveals the fine art of institutional plant smuggling. Kew played a vital role as a transfer point for the commercial exploitation of plants that would contribute to the wealth of the British Empire. By the early nineteenth century the decks of naval ships and East Indiamen were fitted out with glass houses known as "plant cabins" for the shipment of live plant material, which included orchids. Egyptian cotton seed, coffee, and cocoa were sent to West Africa. Sisal hemp went to British East Africa. Cinchona (a source of quinine for the treatment of malaria) was carried from South America to India and Ceylon. Macadamia nuts went from Queensland to Asia and the West Indies. Cork oaks were dispatched to the Punjab region of India, and West African oil palms ended up in Australia, Jamaica, and Singapore. By the end of the nineteenth century Kew had become a powerhouse in the worldwide trafficking of plant material and seeds.

When it came to government-sanctioned theft of the botanical resources of other countries, Kew was in a class all its own. Through its programs of collecting, cataloguing, sales, and distribution of plant material, Kew's commercial interests included opium, tobacco, tropical fruits, and an endless list of ornamental shrubs and flowering plants, including rare tropical orchids. Through these and other efforts, Kew attained a preeminent position in the world with its achievements in the fields of economic botany, horticulture, and scientific research. In those days, the commercial exploitation of plant material and scientific study were thought to be mutually beneficial. Until recently, European botanical institutions have been almost entirely dependent on commercial collectors to bring them new species of orchids and other plants of economic value. This is no longer the case because now there is a line drawn between the commercial and scientific use of these plants. Within the scientific community there is a further distinction made between the work of independent botanists and institutional botanists. Many people in the orchid world have pointed out that the general trend seems to be aimed at curtailing the commercial trade in wild-collected species, and bringing all scientific study, publications, and even the legal naming of species under the control of established institutions. Botanists in developing countries call this type of behavior scientific imperialism, because they feel that they should be the ones who determine how their plant resources are studied and utilized for both scientific and commercial use.

The reason I have included this background on Kew is not to criticize the institution or to belittle the immense value of its scientific work or the worldwide economic benefits that are a direct result of its efforts. I mention the history of Kew for the sole purpose of trying to convey the sense of unreality that I experienced while sitting in Dr. Cribb's office listening to him voice his concerns about plant collectors roaming the world in search of valuable orchids, about orchid seed and pollen smugglers, and about renegade taxonomists and collectors who violate the rights of countries that want to protect their genetic resources. As if unaware of his own institution's history, he expressed contempt for those who would flout international law, and exploit the world's botanical treasures for financial gain.

Returning to the Kew Archives on my last day, I discovered some interesting details about the connection between the Royal Botanic Gardens and Henry Azadehdel. A helpful assistant was kind enough to photocopy a stack of these papers, and that afternoon I walked through the main gate of Kew with information that I had not anticipated. There was even a letter to Henry Azadehdel dated September 11, 1984, requesting the new Chinese species *Paphiopedilum malipoense*. The note was written on Kew stationery and signed by Dr. Cribb.

These and other papers had been presented in court during the appeal phase of Henry Azadehdel's trial. As I read them, I couldn't help thinking that Sir Joseph Banks, the Hookers, and William T. Thiselton-Dyer would have tipped their hats to

Henry and given him their heartfelt blessings. The documents confirmed that Henry had sent significant quantities of rare, wild-collected tropical orchids to Kew, which they had accepted; and it was largely due to this evidence that he was released from prison.

Chapter 14

THE FORBIDDEN FLOWERS
OF GUNNAR SEIDENFADEN

Dendrobium lanyaiae

I was asleep in my compartment when the overnight train from Amsterdam arrived in Copenhagen at dawn. I splashed water on my face, gathered up my bag, and switched trains for the journey north to Elsinore, where I phoned Dr. Gunnar Seidenfaden to let him know I had arrived. He sent a car, and as I waited for it to arrive I fretted about where I would sleep that night. In a letter to Dr. Seidenfaden, who was in his late eighties, I had asked if there was a small hotel near his home where I could stay during my three-day visit to talk about orchids. He wrote back telling me that he could probably find room for me at his home, but I still felt uneasy about imposing myself on an elderly stranger.

Before long, a car pulled up in front of the Elsinore train station. From the driver's side of the vehicle I noticed a very pretty woman waving to me. This was Katja, Dr. Seidenfaden's secretary. She spoke excellent English, and as we drove down the two-lane road into a countryside of undulating green hills and scattered farmhouses, she told me that Gunnar was looking forward to my visit. We rolled down the windows; a warm summer breeze filled the car with the smell of freshly cut hay. We talked about Dr. Seidenfaden and his work with orchids, but when I mentioned my concern about where to stay, Katja just laughed and told me not to worry.

We followed a meandering route to the village of Hornbaek, where we turned onto a long, narrow road flanked by towering shade trees. At the turnoff I noticed a very small sign that read "Borsholmgard." It was not until a cluster of magnificent stone barns and a stately residence came into view that I realized we were on a private drive leading to Dr. Seidenfaden's country estate, which was called Borsholmgard. We pulled to a halt in front of the house, Katja turned off the motor, and we stepped into a large, sunny courtyard fragrant with ancient climbing roses. Beyond the farm buildings and nearby shade trees, a dirt road led into adjacent fields where a tractor was followed by a small cloud of dust.

"You were expecting something else?" Katja laughed.

A housekeeper appeared at the front door of the main residence. She greeted us, and after a brief conversation with the woman Katja said good-bye and returned to her car. Walking into the coolness of the entry hall, I expected to meet Dr. Seidenfaden, but the housekeeper told me that he was taking his midday nap. The woman showed me to my quarters, which turned out to be an entire upstairs wing of the house that overlooked part of a lake and a large garden of lawns, shade trees, shrubs, and tastefully laid-out flowerbeds. In the hallway outside my bedroom, I examined a series of framed black-and-white photographs of Dr. Seidenfaden in the forests of northern Thailand. It must have been quite a journey considering the number of hill tribesmen working as porters. One photograph showed Dr. Seidenfaden with a giant python; another caught him seated at a folding camp table, where he was closely examining a small plant or an insect with a magnifying glass.

To fill in time, I browsed in a downstairs library, where I happened upon an extremely rare first edition of *The Voyage of Governor Arthur Phillip to Botany Bay*. Printed in 1789, it is an account of the 1787–88 voyage of "the First Fleet" and the settlement of convicts in Australia. The book had been presold by subscription, as was common in those days, and I could hardly contain the excitement of holding a first edition in my hands. The feel and smell of the binding and pages and the sight of the marbled boards and spine gilt were enough to send me back more than two hundred years in time. In the 1980s I lived in Sydney for three years. During that time I had heard of this book, but I had never seen a copy until that afternoon in Dr. Seidenfaden's library. There were folding maps and charts and engraved plates of Botany Bay, along with illustrations of nineteen birds, nine mammals, one lizard, four fish, two Aborigines, and one plant (which was not an orchid). I settled into an overstuffed chair in a sunny corner of the library and spent the next several hours lost in thought about the early history of European settlement in Sydney Harbor. By late afternoon, Dr. Seidenfaden had still not made his appearance and I was beginning to wonder if he was feeling well enough to receive guests. I had come to talk with Dr. Seidenfaden because he was in some sort of trouble over live orchid specimens that were being mailed to him from Bangkok. Months earlier, Dr. Seidenfaden had sent me a packet of information to help familiarize me with his work, and as I sat in his library, I reread a copy of a letter that had been written in 1993 by Gren Lucas, the keeper of the herbarium and library at Kew. It was a letter of support to help Dr. Seidenfaden out of an unusual predicament.

The letter explained that Dr. Seidenfaden was the acknowledged world expert on the orchids of Thailand and Southeast Asia, and that he had devoted his life to the study of these plants with the full cooperation and blessings of the countries concerned. Professor Lucas went on to say that Dr. Seidenfaden's publications and research, over fifty years, had provided the foundation of knowledge for the orchids that grow in that part of the world. He further pointed out that Dr. Seidenfaden's work was an essential part of conservation and that it was unrelated to the illegal commercial trade in orchids. He also mentioned that because of a lack of expertise in the region, it should come as no surprise that botanists and students occasionally sent Dr. Seidenfaden specimens for identification. The letter went on to explain how Professor Lucas and Dr. Seidenfaden were selected to help with the formation of CITES in Washington in 1973. In conclusion, he expressed sincere hope that Dr. Seidenfaden would be permitted to freely continue his important work in the field of orchid conservation.

Beyond the information contained in this letter, I knew little about Dr. Seidenfaden apart from the fact that he had served as Danish ambassador to Thailand in the 1950s and that two genera of orchids, *Gunnarella* and *Seidenfadenia,* were named after him.

At around 4 P.M. an elderly man holding a cane and a clear plastic bag full of dried bread appeared at the doorway to the library. This was Dr. Seidenfaden, and in a rather feeble voice he announced that he was ready to go feed the ducks. The old man could hardly walk, so I carried the bread as we slowly made our way to the lake. Once we were safely seated on a bench at the edge of the water, my host proceeded to fill me in on the marital intrigues of his three wild ducks. By Dr. Seidenfaden's reckoning, the male had rejected his original mate because no ducklings had been produced. A second wife was brought to the pond, but the result of this union met with similar results.

"Haaaah! Still no ducklings," chortled Gunnar. "It is my opinion that the problem might be the result of a deficiency on the part of this feathered gentleman."

He then told me a series of duck stories, based on his observations over the previous several months, and instructed me on the fine art of throwing pieces of dried bread into the lake. When the ducks came closer, Dr. Seidenfaden began quacking, and the ducks quacked back. A lengthy exchange of duck talk ensued. It was at about this point that I started thinking about the possibility of catching the next train back to Copenhagen the following morning. Our duck-feeding duties completed, I took Dr. Seidenfaden's arm and helped him back to the house, where he promptly disappeared until dinner time. After a quiet meal Dr. Seidenfaden excused himself from the table, but asked me to join him in his study at 10 P.M.

By the time Dr. Seidenfaden reappeared I hardly recognized him. He wore a crisply ironed dress shirt with a silk ascot arranged at the collar. He was freshly shaved, alert, and animated, and there was absolutely no trace of the faltering old man I had taken to the duck pond that afternoon. He reached for a well-seasoned briar pipe and before long the room was filled with the sweet, pungent smell of good-quality pipe tobacco.

"I get started a bit later in the day than I used to," Gunnar explained, as he poured two glasses of port. Ten P.M. was the beginning of his workday, and for the next three nights we met in his study at the same hour to talk and drink port until around two or three in the morning.

Sitting at his desk, Gunnar was the centerpiece of a wood-paneled study filled with mementos and gifts from his travels around the world. A huge python skin (the one from the photograph upstairs) was partially obscured by a collection of Southeast Asian sun hats, spears, crossbows, swords, and machetes. A Burmese umbrella that smelled of waxed canvas, musical instruments, framed documents, photographs, and botanical prints covered the walls between tall bookshelves stuffed with leather-bound volumes and an assortment of storage cabinets. Amid the orderly chaos of this well-used workplace sat a carved statue of Ganesh, the jovial Hindu elephant god, and another of Shiva.

It was a cozy office. A vase of freshly cut roses sat to one side of the cluttered desktop, where half-finished pencil sketches of orchid flower segments lay spread on the green leather writing surface. Knotted rugs covered a herringbone pattern of oak floorboards and a steam radiator hissed beneath tall windows that overlooked the darkened gravel courtyard. A microscope, rolls of drawing paper, stacks of letters from foreign countries, various magnifying glasses, and back issues of the *Times Literary Supplement* and the *Economist* were scattered along with pots of flowering orchids. In the basement Gunnar kept more than 10,000 meticulously labeled orchid specimens preserved in alcohol, while elsewhere in the large, rambling house he stored "his papers"—a vast archive of personal correspondence and scientific data.

Gunnar started his travels as a young man in the summer of 1928, when he joined a series of scientific expeditions to Greenland. He was a student of natural history at the University of Copenhagen at the time, but for the next few summers he spent so much time in Greenland that he never got around to memorizing the names of Danish wildflowers. Thanks to this botanical shortcoming, he failed his exams and ended up studying political science. In 1934 Gunnar went to Thailand to visit his uncle, Erik Seidenfaden, who was working there as an ethnologist. Gunnar stayed for six months, during which time he became interested in orchids. His fascination with these plants endured over the years, and by the time he returned to Thailand as the Danish ambassador in 1955 he was ready to embark on a series of collecting trips and start his systematic study of Southeast Asian orchids. In 1965 Gunnar co-authored *The Orchids of Thailand* with his friend Tem Smitinand, who worked for the Royal Thai Forest Department. Gunnar told me that the black-and-white photographs in the hallway outside my bedroom were from the fourth Thai-Danish Botanical Expedition in 1963, which was one of his last journeys into the remote rain forests of northern Thailand.

During our conversation the first night, Gunnar explained how he had worked for the Danish Ministry of the Environment for many years after retiring from the Ministry of Foreign Affairs. He represented Denmark at international conferences on pollution in the Baltic Sea, and he was considered an expert on the various environmental threats to the flora and fauna of Europe. In 1973 he was selected as the orchid expert who helped draft the original CITES legislation to protect endangered plants. He was so highly regarded by the Danish government that the Ministry of the Environment named the flagship of their fleet MS *Gunnar Seidenfaden*.

One of the first things I wanted to discuss with Dr. Seidenfaden was his involvement with the creation of CITES and how plants were included in the treaty. Gunnar explained how in the beginning the IUCN in Switzerland, which includes NGOs and governments, decided that it might be able to aid conservation by controlling wildlife trade across international borders. He pointed out that this was a trade agreement, not a conservation agreement, regarding species that are threatened by extinction.

"So the Washington Convention of 1973 was called," Gunnar said, "but it was originally about animals, not plants. Flora was suddenly introduced about a fortnight before the meeting. A last-minute decision had determined that wildlife must also include flora. As it turned out, no provisions had been made for the flora side of things. Few botanists were at the conference. Just Gren Lucas from Kew, myself, and a few others. The rest were foreign affairs and governmental ministers and so forth. The botanists all agreed that there were too few of us and that we knew too little about the whole thing to be able to build up the flora side of the treaty during the meeting. At the end of the convention we stated that flora was poorly treated in the convention because we were not given adequate time to prepare. We could also see a lot of problems in the treaty. We said that the countries signing the treaty should have the CITES sectretariat work out the flora side, but that was never done. Flora has just been hung on the animal regulations the whole time."

Dr. Seidenfaden went on to discuss how things evolved at CITES meetings after the Washington Convention. "At these meetings they talk about turtles and alligators and bats and tigers and they talk very little about flora. The whole thing was taken over by administration people, especially by the European Common Market, and these people were lawyers, not scientists. We should have protested that each country should have a CITES managing authority as well as a scientific authority, and then made sure that they complemented each other. In Denmark we have no scientific authority. None. Never made one, and that was one big error. So this meant that the thing has been driven forward by the bureaucrats in Brussels—people who make all these legalistic rules without taking into consideration the basic facts of botany. And so I got out of it and don't participate in the meetings that they have every two years. But from their recent publications it is quite clear that there is some improvement in the field of flora. They are now beginning to understand that what they have done is absolutely wrong."

In recent years Gunnar had mostly devoted himself to entertaining his grandchildren with stories about giant snakes, encounters with tigers, and the history of Southeast Asia, but he also spent his time writing a new book on the orchids of Thailand. To assist him in this work, young students, botanists, and commercial orchid growers in Thailand, India, and Europe sent him orchid specimens for identification, and it was these shipments of live plant material that led to Gunnar's legal problems.

"As a scientist," said Gunnar, "I live in constant fear that the authorities are going to completely stop the worldwide exchange of orchids that are of scientific interest. Oh, they are nasty people, and I don't care for them at all."

The Danish customs officials were constantly seizing his mail when it contained orchid specimens, and he had little recourse but to let them confiscate the plants. Gunnar explained how the orchids were all taken to "a concentration camp for plants where they died a slow death from abuse and neglect." Many of these orchids had been sent to Gunnar by young university students, and quite often the plants turned out to be new species. Under Danish law, this sort of scientific exchange of plants was illegal. Gunnar was frustrated and bewildered by the misinterpretation of CITES conservation regulations that he had helped to create twenty-four years earlier. In a letter dated May 10, 1992, addressed to Eric Hagsater, then chairman of the IUCN World Conservation Union Orchid Specialist Group, he complained that CITES had developed into a bureaucratic police force dominated by lawyers who knew nothing about plants and who were obsessed with "legalistic refinement and juridical sophistry."

"The Convention never intended to destroy the international cooperation between scientists," Gunnar explained. "I am not a trader who threatens plants. I am a scientist trying to help conservation by finding out what kind of orchids we have in the world. That is my job."

I asked Gunnar for details about his present difficulties. He explained that despite CITES guidelines that permit member countries to exempt scientists and scientific institutions from the cumbersome commercial import-export permit requirements, the Danish government had decided not to do so. And even if there were a Scientific CITES permit system in Denmark, the young students and commercial orchid growers in Thailand and elsewhere would also need a Scientific CITES permit (which they are not entitled to) in order to export the plants. Gunnar pointed out that all scientific exchanges of plant specimens in Denmark go on without CITES documents. "Because of this idiocy, all botanists in Denmark are now living in sin, but it is the only way to do our work," said Gunnar.

One night he told me an interesting story about a scientific exchange between botanists that took place in October 1981. Ger van Vliet, then the director of the Botanic Garden at the University of Leiden in the Netherlands, along with Ed de Vogel (the same botanist who several years later assisted Phillip Cribb during the armed raid on Popow's orchid nursery in Germany), drove to Gunnar's home in search of live orchids to add to the coelogyne-bulbophyllum collection at Leiden.

"Van Vliet came with Ed de Vogel," Gunnar recalled, "and they brought a bottle of this Dutch hard spirits called Genever. I prefer a good Bordeaux, but in any event I took them into my orchid house in Copenhagen and we picked out all the plant material they wanted. They got everything that they were looking for, that is for sure! The orchids went into a very big plastic bag which they sent back to the Netherlands."

I asked Gunnar what would happen if I took a similar bag full of orchids across the border. Would it be legal? I wondered.

"I should think not," said Gunnar, "because it is taking CITES-regulated plant material across two international borders. The Danish customs people would want to see a CITES export permit and that is something van Vliet and I never discussed. He just filled the bag with my plants and that was that. Now that we are all members of the Common Market, there are no customs agents at the border to check these things, but this doesn't mean that it is legal. Ever since around 1770 there has been a free exchange of plants between Denmark and Leiden, and this sort of trading has gone on since the study of orchids began, until CITES came along. We used to send hundreds of plant specimens to foreign museums and botanic gardens for them to study. We would get plants from them in return and this is the way it should be. It is a very old tradition that went on for centuries, but now it is illegal."

Five months after his return to the Netherlands, Ger van Vliet wrote Gunnar a very nice thank-you note, along with a detailed list of the plants that had safely arrived at the Botanic Garden at Leiden for propagation and de Vogel's research. He also mentioned which ones had flowered and produced seed.

Several years passed before Gunnar started having difficulties importing orchid specimens for his research. A woman, whom Gunnar would only refer to as "the Iron Lady," had taken complete control of the CITES Management Authority in

Denmark. Her primary interest was in maintaining Danish farm subsidies from the European Union office in Brussels, but she also exercised considerable control over the Danish orchid-growing community and was making things difficult for commercial growers and botanists like Gunnar. By this time van Vliet had moved on to become the plants officer at the CITES headquarters near Geneva. He had become one of the most powerful people in the world for influencing the international trade in rare plants. So Gunnar called on his old friend and colleague to see if there was something that might be done to help defend the rights of Danish botanists. In his written response, van Vliet told him that it was up to the Danish authorities, and that Gunnar would just have to follow the rules.

"Rules?" laughed Gunnar. "What nonsense! Let me tell you a story about Dr. van Vliet and the rules." Gunnar became very animated during this part of our discussion as the old memories came back to him. He poured out two more glasses of port and then continued with his story.

"In the mid-1980s I started work on the identification of a Thai orchid that looked very similar to *Brachypeza laotica*. I had only a few loose dead flowers to work from, which was not enough for me to complete my investigation, or to determine if it was a new species. So in June 1992 I wrote to my friend Mr. Suphachadiwong, who is a very reputable orchid dealer in Bangkok. I asked him if he could send me a live specimen of the plant for study. Mr. Suphachadiwong wrote back to tell me that until recently, he had sixteen plants, but he could not send me any of them because he had just received a visit from a man from CITES by the name of van Vliet."

Gunnar went on to explain that van Vliet had told Mr. Suphachadiwong that if he wanted to be a "friend" of CITES, he must immediately stop all export of wild-collected orchids. Mr. Suphachadiwong agreed to this, but when he asked van Vliet what he should do with the sixteen orchid specimens that had already been collected, van Vliet told the nurseryman to send all of the plants to the Botanic Garden in Leiden. In May 1992 Mr. Suphachadiwong "donated" all of the plants to Leiden.

When I asked Dr. van Vliet about the details of this story, he wrote back, denying any involvement. He also told me that he could see no reason to comment on an interpretation by Dr. Seidenfaden or any other person. His reply also included a rather pugnacious "It will be very interesting to see how much fact and fiction is in your book." In a letter dated June 24, 1993, written by Heike Suphachadiwong to Dr. Seidenfaden regarding the missing *Brachypeza laotica,* he clearly states: ". . . in May last year, we have donated Thai orchid species to the Botanic Garden in Leiden. . . . The contact was made by Dr. Ger van Vliet, plant officer of the CITES Secretariat."

But this was not the end of the story. Gunnar was very disappointed at not being able to complete his work because of lack of plant material, so he wrote to the Botanic Garden at Leiden to request one of the purloined plants. Either a live plant or a dried herbarium specimen would do. The people at Leiden never gave Gunnar a live plant, but they eventually sent him one dead flower preserved in alcohol.

"Oh, this is a frightful business!" Gunnar exclaimed.

This was only the beginning of Gunnar's problems with the authorities. Six months before I visited him, the Danish Ministry of the Environment was trying to encourage Gunnar to surrender a Thai orchid that had been sent to him without a proper permit. Gunnar told the authorities that they would have to take him to court if they wanted to get the plant. This apparently frightened the midlevel people at the ministry because Gunnar was a friend of the minister of the environment, who had already made it clear that it was out of the question to prosecute someone of Dr. Seidenfaden's stature over such a trivial issue.

"So the head of the prosecution came up with a solution," Gunnar said. "He invited me to his office for a very nice lunch and after this lunch, he asked me to just hand over the plant to the authorities and then they could drop the case. I told them that I was willing to write a letter to them admitting that I was a sinner and that they could have the plant, but only on the condition that they send it back to me for safekeeping. They agreed to this, so I let them confiscate the plant, which they returned to me a few days later so that I could get it to flower and decide what it was."

By this time, the story of Gunnar's forbidden flower was starting to get into the local newspapers. When it came to the attention of the minister of the environment, he said that the harassment of Dr. Seidenfaden had to be stopped immediately. A short while later Gunnar was invited to another lunch to discuss the situation; while he was at lunch an "orchid expert" arrived at Gunnar's greenhouse to get the orchid. Gunnar speculated that the man wanted to destroy it, because without the plant there would be no court case. Luckily for Gunnar, he had a very smart young woman working for him who told the "orchid expert" she was very busy and that he would have to find the plant by himself. There were 2,000 or 3,000 orchids in the greenhouse and the "expert" was unable to locate the plant, even though it was sitting on the table in front of him. When Gunnar discovered what had happened, he wrote a letter of protest to the Ministry of the Environment accusing them of trying to kill a plant that, by law, they were required to protect. He also wanted to know what any of this silly business had to do with protecting or conserving rare plants.

Gunnar finally signed a detailed agreement with the Ministry of the Environment that allowed him to receive orchids for scientific study. The agreement limited his use of the plants and granted ownership of the orchids to the ministry. The orchids could not leave Gunnar's house, they could not be propagated, and the flowers or other plant parts could not be sent to other scientists for any purpose.

"They are shooting cannonballs at mosquitoes. It is all so absurd and I have completely given up discussing the matter with them. I have promised not to do certain things, but I do them anyway. The authorities know this, but the written agreement allows them to leave me alone and that is all I care about. I want to end my life working on my book about Thai orchids. I would like to complete it by my ninetieth birthday. Thailand has more than 1,200 orchid species and so there is work to do."

With that comment, Gunnar emptied the bottle of port into our glasses. We had a toast to the success of what would be his final book and then drained the last sweet golden drops. It was after 3 A.M. and I decided to let Gunnar get back to work. I went for a walk across the courtyard to where it led into the darkened fields. Looking back at the house I could see Gunnar at his desk, sketching, typing, and peering into his microscope. In his eighty-eighth year Gunnar felt confident that with luck, good health, and no further distractions from the authorities, there was still enough time to finish his work. Watching him through the window, I found myself hoping he would be granted that blessing of time.

Chapter 15

ORCHIDS, GUNS, AND HARPSICHORDS

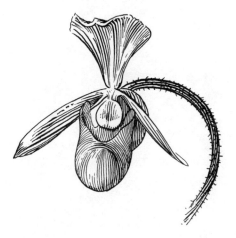

Paphiopedilum helenae

Before his eighteenth birthday, in 1996, Xavier Garreau de Loubresse achieved cult status in the orchid world with his large collection of extremely rare species. He had worked with the legendary French orchid growers Maurice and Marcel Lecoufle, but like many of the rising stars in the orchid world Xavier was mostly self-taught. He also proved to be quite adept at igniting feelings of admiration and rage from colleagues and total strangers.

A Dutch orchid grower, envious of Xavier's growing reputation and influence, bitterly accused him of being "an arrogant, opinionated, and paranoid brat." An elderly German nurseryman referred to Xavier as "a visionary and a genius," and then added that the young man owed huge sums of money to orchid growers in Thailand, the Philippines, Germany, and the United States. Customs officials in Paris refer to Xavier as *l'enfant terrible* of the orchid world, but they generally approve of his orchid-growing activities and have given him remarkable freedom to import plants for breeding purposes and scientific study. From these conflicting accounts it was clear that regardless of whether people approved or disapproved of Xavier, there was little doubt that he was an orchid fanatic of the first order.

Blind rage, crippling jealousy, and wild exaggeration are commonplace in the quirky and insular world of orchid growing, but nothing that I had heard over the previous five years prepared me for the rumors about Xavier. It was perplexing how such a young man could generate so much controversy and vicious gossip. One account had him living with thousands of rare orchids and his mother in a Belle Époque apartment in the sixteenth arrondissement of Paris. According to the source, every window and wall of the apartment was covered with fungi because of the humid greenhouse conditions. The rooms were filled with a jungle of rare tropical orchids that covered the floors and tables and hung from the tall ceilings. I was told that when Xavier wasn't watering his plants or spraying them with toxic chemicals, he played the harpsichord for guests or fired bullets into the walls of his bedroom. Rumor went so far as to describe how his mother slept with a pump-action sawed-off shotgun. I didn't believe a word of this nonsense, but in the back of my mind I prayed that at least some of it was true. In any case, I couldn't wait to meet Xavier and his mother.

An orchid dealer from England gave me the street address and telephone number of Xavier's apartment in Paris. The man sketched a map showing the layout of the apartment, and wrote down the security code for the front door of the building. I had absolutely no intention of entering the apartment of an armed orchid grower without an invitation; but the fact that a total stranger would give me this detailed information made me wonder about Xavier's previous business dealings with the man. For more than a year I tried to contact Xavier through letters and e-mail, but he would not respond. I tried flattery, and offered habitat and cultural information on Borneo orchid species that I knew he was interested in. I lied by telling him I was interested in guns, but nothing I said broke his silence. People in the orchid business in Paris told me Xavier had gone underground because of his debts, and for this reason he would never talk to me.

I called my orchid-growing friend, Eleanor Kerrigan of Seattle, for advice on how to tempt the young Frenchman out of hiding. I hoped that she would know what to do, but after I told her what I knew about Xavier and gave my reasons for wanting to meet him, she promptly told me that I had gone off the deep end. "Orchid fever. That's what you've got, boy, and you've got it bad," she laughed.

Eleanor hung up the phone, and as I listened to the dial tone I finally had to admit that the orchids were doing strange things to me. By the time I started searching for Xavier, I had spent more than five years roaming the lunatic fringe of the orchid world. In the beginning, I just wanted to find out how beautiful flowers could be responsible for so much vile behavior. It didn't take long to get a taste of what was going on. By the time I discovered that many convicted "smugglers" were true conservationists, and that certain well-positioned "conservationists" were smuggling plants with the help of fake CITES permits for "scientific study," I knew where the action was. I zeroed in on these characters, and the more convoluted their stories sounded, the more eagerly I hunted them down.

I couldn't remember the last time I had looked at a flower and appreciated it for its fragile beauty. Orchids had become trigger mechanisms. The sight of the magnificent flower of *Paphiopedilum supardii* brought to mind a petty taxonomic feud between two botanists, while *Cattleya violacea* reminded me of an orchid grower from Minnesota who once confessed that he wore mirrored sunglasses year-round because they made it easier for him to stare at women's breasts. *Paphiopedilum greyi* Thunder Thighs conjured up the image of very large orchid judges eating chocolate-covered doughnuts, and *Sedirea japon-*

ica made me think of the fragrance designer Joe Heydel, who made his living sniffing orchids. At one point, I was so strung out that I could not look at one of these plants without some screwball orchid personality leaping into my thoughts. The sight of *Paphiopedilum sanderianum* made me think of the orchid hunter Donald Levitt perched atop his collapsible, camouflaged cardboard toilet on the slopes of Fire Mountain. Even in the checkout line of my neighborhood grocery store there was no escape from the orchid people. Behind the cash register sat a long shelf filled with mass-produced *Phalaenopsis* hybrids, selling for $19.95; every time I saw them I thought about the California orchid grower who shot and killed his partner and then mutilated the corpse because they couldn't agree on how to breed and sell these supermarket-quality house plants.

I don't want to give the impression that perfectly normal, healthy, thoughtful, and balanced people are not drawn to orchids. I am told they exist. I just didn't have much luck finding them. The ones I encountered were the horticultural extremists, the lone rangers, pioneers, fantasy merchants, and traveling flower show flim-flam people. They were like irresistible wildflowers, and I collected them at every opportunity. Jumbled in my mind were paid informers, rapacious nurserymen, international plant smugglers, pollen thieves, eccentric botanists, corrupt orchid judges, legendary collectors and growers, misfits, groupies, and camp followers galore.

Once in a very great while I had the pleasure of meeting people like Michael and Teresa Fung, of Maisie Orchids, who simply loved their plants and nurtured them in a way that evoked feelings of pleasure and serenity. There were home growers and hobbyists who turned a blind eye to plant politics and pursued their passion for orchids with a depth of feeling and commitment that continues to astonish me. I also had the pleasure of meeting great spirits like Gunnar Seidenfaden, who radiated an intense vitality and love of life. Gunnar is a voice of reason in the wilderness; a person who, with a single anecdote, can reduce to rubble decades of multimillion-dollar, misguided, and self-serving conservation efforts—and do so without malice.

But more often than not, I found myself with people like the dried-fox-testicle–orchid-tuber ice cream makers of eastern Turkey, or the geriatric orchid breeder from Los Angeles who sat in his "Stud Room" drinking straight shots of Wild Turkey while he chortled to himself, listened to rock-and-roll oldies on the radio, and had toothpick sex with his orchids. And then there was the born-again Christian orchid retailer from Wisconsin who told me how he spent his midwinter Sunday mornings stretched out naked on a table in the greenhouse. Bathed in the damp heat, he drank amaretto-flavored instant cappuccino and listened to the sort of New Age ambient music that consists of whale and dolphin squeaks, underwater bubbles, flushing toilets, shorebird calls, pseudo–Native American drumming, and the kind of flute melodies that work just like Valium, but have fewer harmful side effects.

Every time I looked at a pressed orchid herbarium specimen I thought of Dr. Braem fist-fighting with German customs officials over dead plants collected in the nineteenth century. My obsession with the orchid world got to the point where I could not walk into a greenhouse without envisioning the place swarming with Kevlar-vested, stun-grenade-throwing, armed customs officers and their attack dogs. It was a crazy, whacked-out group of people, and whether I liked it or not, I could not get enough of them. I had become a junkie for their stories, and that is why I needed to find Xavier.

A year went by after my first attempts to contact Xavier, and during that time I continued to amuse myself and friends with the image of a harpsichord-playing orchid grower who ingested large amounts of toxic insecticides and spent his leisure time firing bullets into the walls of his bedroom. This vision was suddenly shattered in late 1998 when I received an unexpected letter from Xavier. He apologized for his long silence and explained how his orchid work had suffered a series of setbacks. He was just starting up a new propagation lab and wondered if I was still interested in meeting him. We set a date, but the very thought of confronting my fantasy version of him left me in a cold sweat.

Nervous about the likelihood that none of the delectable rumors had been true, I flew to Paris in early January 1999 to meet Xavier and his mother, Michelle Garreau de Loubresse-Corlin. The three of us had lunch at Au Pied de Cochon, a restaurant near Les Halles on the rue Coquillerè. My first impression of Xavier was disappointing. He seemed to be a perfectly well-mannered, articulate, decent, and highly intelligent young man, and these qualities were in sharp contrast to what I had hoped for. His mother was also very different from what I had expected. She was young, well dressed, and had a quiet and bemused manner that I found very attractive. Sitting at the table, an uneasy feeling came over me as I realized it was quite possible that I was the strange one.

We ordered choucroute with a chilled Alsatian Riesling, and within minutes Xavier had covered the entire table with color photos of his orchid collection. While we were examining the photographs, the waiter brought a massive platter piled high with cumin-scented boiled pigs' knuckles, blood sausage, steaming potatoes, and braised sauerkraut. Xavier cleared a small area for the platter, and through the clouds of steam that arose from the cabbage I could make out the familiar forms of exotic *Paphiopedilum* species, including *delenatii, rothschildianum, stonei,* and *sanderianum.* But what caught my attention were the photos of more recently discovered slipper orchids, of which *Paphiopedilum helenae, P. jackii,* and *P. gigantifolium* were in full bloom. Xavier knew the precise latitude and longitude of where these last three plants grew in the wild, the names of the men who had collected them, the prices paid, and details of how the plants had moved across international borders. Listening to this information, I realized that Xavier was no pretender. He knew what he was talking about.

With eyeglasses fogged from the steaming sauerkraut, Xavier told me about his world, and long before the first pig's knuckle was reduced to glistening bone and cartilage, I realized that the rumors about him barely scratched the surface. For the next seven hours Xavier talked, and during that time I discovered that the stories about the apartment filled with orchids, the guns, the harpsichord, and the bullet holes in his bedroom wall were true. The highlights of his gun collection included several M98K Mauser rifles, an Uzi, and the original prototype of the German Luger machine pistol. When asked about the bullet holes, he explained that they were "an accident, the result of a non-orchid-related problem."

Non-orchid-related problem? I liked the tantalizing hint of unknown violence, but I resisted the temptation to ask whether, by any chance, the bullets might have passed through a human body during their brief journey from gun barrel to wall.

Moving on to lighter topics, Xavier told me that he first started growing orchids when he was eleven years old. At the age of fifteen he had won a special scientific award at the World

Orchid Conference in Glasgow for his research into producing seed capsules from cut flower stems. Xavier dropped out of school at sixteen because, as his mother explained, he was being harassed by the teachers and the other pupils. Once he left school he devoted himself full time to the cultivation and study of orchids. Within two years he had accumulated an impressive collection of rare orchids. His lab work using coconut water (a natural liquid endosperm) in his growth media to help germinate seeds started to attract the attention and envy of many influential people in the orchid world. He became part of an exclusive group of growers, traders, smugglers, informers, and scientists whose loyalties were as fragile and unpredictable as the orchids they worked with.

During lunch, Xavier provided me with an avalanche of details about the turf battles being fought among Dutch, German, French, and Taiwanese orchid growers, and how the yakusa (Japanese mobsters), Hong Kong Triads, and Colombian drug lords laundered money with rare orchids. I was uncertain about how much of this to believe, but there was little time for reflection that afternoon. Xavier went on to explain how large shipments of orchids and other rare plants were being moved across the docks of Marseilles without customs formalities. He spoke enthusiastically of the development of a new scanner that would be able to detect water molecules and identify smuggled plants in airport luggage. Xavier knew which growers, scientists, and customs officials were under investigation, and of course his monologue was peppered with bizarre anecdotes. One of my favorites had to do with a group of jovial customs officials from Austria. According to Xavier, they had developed such a low opinion of a CITES official in Geneva that each Christmas they sent the man a beautifully wrapped gift box full of dog shit. Included with the gift was a thank-you note praising the official for his continuing efforts to protect endangered plant species.

Xavier explained how the orchid world was crawling with informants. "In France alone," he said, "there are seventy-three numbered and paid informers, and they are entitled to 10 or 20 percent of any fine with a $200,000 cap on any one operation." When I jokingly asked him if he had seen any surveillance information on me, he told me of a "Suspect File" that he had seen in Brussels. The report mentioned my frequent visits to Borneo over the years, and included a partial list of people I had traveled with. This came as a bit of a shock (I later managed to exchange a bit of my own information for a look at a hand-written synopsis of the report, which included the name of its author). Despite this delectable tidbit of information, I am still uncertain about the accuracy of many of Xavier's stories.

When I asked Xavier if he was still growing orchids in his apartment, he told me that he had moved his collection to a new location on the outskirts of Paris three months earlier. Opinions vary about the use of fungicides and insecticides; many growers believe these chemicals should be used sparingly. But Xavier felt that orchids needed to be treated approximately every two weeks with products that are definitely not healthy for humans. Over a five-year period he had sprayed more than twenty liters of toxic chemicals in the apartment he shared with his mother and the orchids, and this had sent his red bloodcell count plummeting.

"I use organophosphate insecticides," Xavier explained. "One of them is known as dimethylphosphorodithiaic acid, which can be dangerous if you don't use it properly. Organophosphates can affect the brain stem and for the last couple of years

I have had health problems. The insecticide interferes with enzymes in the nervous systems of insect pests and then causes death by paralysis of the respiratory system. I'm not sure what my other sprays can do to humans, but when the boy living downstairs started losing his hair and vomiting uncontrollably, I figured it was time to move the orchids to a new location."

Reading up on the general history and health hazards of organophosphate insecticides, I came upon the book *Virus Hunter*, by C. J. Peters and Mark Olshaker. A passage that caught my interest had to do with how, in 1939, the German scientist Dr. Gerhard Schrader was working on a new organophosphate insecticide when he came up with the novel idea of developing a nerve gas to kill people rather than insects. Who can say where this sort of inspiration comes from, but he soon developed Tuban, the first nerve gas. Tuban wasn't quite lethal enough for Dr. Schrader's liking, so he continued his work for an additional two years until he created his masterpiece, a nerve agent that we now know as Sarin. Organophosphate insecticides work the same way as Sarin. This made me wonder about the state of Xavier's brain stem.

After lunch, Xavier, Madame de Loubresse-Corlin, and I walked to the nearest Metro station, where we caught a series of trains that took us to the outskirts of Paris. I am still uncertain in which direction we traveled, but after about forty-five minutes we got out of the train and stepped into a car that was waiting for us. I half-expected to be blindfolded in order to keep our final destination secret, but five minutes later we pulled to the curbside in a quiet, middle-class neighborhood. At the doorway of a nondescript suburban house we were met by Dr. Truong Van Thuong, a botanist from Vietnam who was in charge of Xavier's lab and orchid collection. Stepping into the house, I caught my breath as I struck a wall of moist tropical heat. The sensation of coming through the front door was a bit like entering Ali Baba's cave; that is, if Ali Baba had been a grower of rare orchids and kept his cave at 80 degrees Fahrenheit, installed banks of grow lights and an air circulation system, and maintained a relative humidity of around 85 percent.

I was astonished to discover that the entire building had been converted into a multilevel greenhouse. Nursery supplies lay stacked in closets. There was not a stick of furniture or any other domestic item in sight. The façade of the three-story house looked normal, but the entire back section of the building had been transformed into a structure with glass walls on three sides. A confusion of stairways led from one level to the next. Floors and walls had been removed so that natural light flooded a tropical wonderland of exotic orchids set out on long nursery tables. A sophisticated laboratory and seedling nursery were tucked away in an adjoining area, where tier upon tier of glass shelving held tens of thousands of miniature seedlings in sterile flasks. The space was completely silent, with the exception of our own footsteps and the gentle hum of water pumps.

This was Xavier's domain: a fabulous hoard of exotic and rare orchids where he lavished attention on treasures like *Bulbophyllum echinolabium,* the green-flowered *Paphiopedilum jackii,* and one of my favorite Borneo species, *Paphiopedilum rothschildianum.* To my surprise, Xavier was still enraptured by the beautiful plants. He handled the orchids gently and spoke of them with a reverence that was unexpectedly touching. I thought Xavier had been enthusiastic during lunch, but his mood at the restaurant was absolutely somnambulant when compared to his behavior that afternoon. Not wanting me to miss a single plant, he led me from one orchid to the next. He took immense delight in showing off his collection, and as he spoke there was no doubt that these plants were his great passion in life. So great was that passion that long before the conclusion of the tour, my mind had turned to jelly. Xavier's virtuoso performance was unforgettable, but as for the orchids, I can hardly remember more than a few of those magnificent plants.

Dr. Thuong, who had nodded politely but said practically nothing during the tour, drove us back to the train station at sundown. He smiled, shook my hand, and then drove off. We waited for the train in silence. It was dark before Xavier, his mother, and I reached the outskirts of Paris. After the comforting warmth of the greenhouse, I was shivering from the damp cold and numb from what I had seen and heard. The three of us were making our way through a maze of subterranean tunnels, deep in the heart of the Paris Metro system, when Xavier's mother suddenly came to a halt. She thanked me warmly, kissed me on both cheeks, and was soon swept away by a flow of commuters that funneled into a darkened passageway. Xavier and I entered a different passageway, boarded our train, and continued toward the city center. At the Chatelet–Les Halles station, Xavier said good-bye and stepped through the sliding train doors. As the train moved on, I realized how much I enjoyed meeting Xavier. He was intense and complex in a way that fell just short of fanaticism, and this contributed to his unique personality. In a daze, I got off at my stop and wandered back to the hotel that I had left eight hours earlier.

As I climbed the stairs to the hotel room, my head was pounding and my ears rang from the sounds of Latin binomials that still echoed in my mind. I threw off my clothes, drew a steaming bath, and then, like a junkie slumping into a euphoric stupor, I submerged myself in the hot water. Immediately I began to melt. Steaming myself into oblivion, I realized that the orchid habit was going to be a hard one to kick, but for the time being I couldn't have cared less. I was high as a kite on the orchid people, and it felt good.

Meeting Xavier was like discovering the rarest orchid on earth. Completely satiated, I tossed my notebook to the floor of the bathroom and experienced the writer's equivalent of post-coital bliss. The last thing I remember before nodding off was a vision of Xavier. He was probably at home reading a book or having a quiet dinner, but in my mind I saw him surrounded by thousands of orchids, all of them in bloom. Night had fallen. The moon was up, and a light fog of organophosphate insecticide wafted through the candle-lit rooms of a crumbling building, encrusted with fungi and pockmarked with bullet holes. Xavier was seated at a long bench; a machine gun with a smoking barrel lay at his feet, and he was playing the harpsichord.

Chapter 16

TOM NELSON AND
THE BOG ORCHID RESCUE

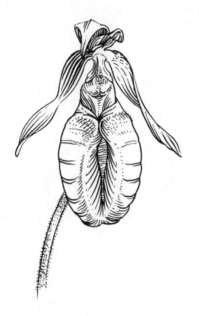

Cypripedium acaule

Northern Minnesota is a land of wolves, moose, snowmobiles, walleye, black bears, black flies, small boats with big engines, monumental fish sculptures, mosquitoes, muskies, and a beer called Fitgers. According to the old-timers, the beer was so vile that only the Finns and the Ojibway Indians would drink the stuff, but in fact Fitgers was the beverage of choice for generations of Minnesotans until the brewery closed a few years back. Judging from a recent survey of the roadside ditches of Lake of the Woods County, Fitgers has now been replaced by Old Milwaukee, Schmidt, and Budweiser.

This borderland area that extends from the northwest shore of Lake Superior to North Dakota is well known for its scenic lakes during the summer. The region is also dotted with black spruce and tamarack fens, shaded woodlands, and peat bogs, which provide prime habitat for many species of spectacular North American terrestrial orchids such as the Minnesota state flower, *Cypripedium reginae,* commonly known as the showy lady's slipper orchid. The other common orchids of northern Minnesota are the moccasin orchid (*Cypripedium acaule*) and the yellow lady's slipper orchid (two subspecies of *C. calceolus*).

Tom Nelson rescues these orchids and other species of woodland perennials from road-building crews and sphagnum moss strip miners. Each year, around late May or early June, when the plants are coming into bloom, Tom can be found, knee-deep in muck, working the roadside ditches with a shovel. Drunken motorists, under the impression that he is scavenging for aluminum cans, have been known to throw their partial empties at him while traveling at high speed.

One afternoon in the summer of 1997, Tom parked his battered panel van, "The Beast," in front of 9 Mile Bar on Highway 169, about nine miles from Grand Rapids. The black flies were biting bad that day and it was time to get out of the sun for a cheeseburger and a bit of conversation. Entering the truck-stop bar, he saw a woman standing in front of the jukebox, singing along to Hank Williams. Her powerful, sweet, lilting voice floated through the bar, soothing the rough edges of hard men and their women. The wall behind the bar was covered with mounted, trophy-sized walleye, northern pike, muskies, a rainbow trout the size of a king salmon, and both largemouth and smallmouth bass. It was a normal midday crowd, and seated at the bar were the likes of Junior Jones, Big Klink, and Timmy White Eagle. A huge man from over Jessie Lake way was trying to sell a portable sawmill with little success. As Tom Nelson described the scene, the smell of stale beer, cigarette smoke, honest sweat, and aftershave wafted through 9 Mile Bar along with the sounds of pool balls and pinball machines. The shelves behind the bar were lined with jars of sausages, pickled turkey gizzards, and hard-boiled eggs immersed in a yellowish liquid. These items looked like ancient laboratory specimens on display, but according to Big Klink, after a sufficient quantity of Fitgers beer, people had been known to put these things in their mouths and eat them. A handwritten sign below the mounted fish read:

HORSESHOE PITS NOW OPEN

The singer sauntered over to the bar stool where Tom was sitting. She placed a foot on the rail, put her hands on her hips, and said, "So . . . you're the orchid man."

"Says who?"

"Small town, long story. Ever seen a white showy?"

"You mean the white-and-pinks?"

"No, the all-whites. The alba form of *Cypripedium reginae*."

"Never seen one. And you?" Tom asked.

"Right outside my kitchen door. My grandmother collected it in 1958. When she died, I got the plant. It's still alive and just bloomed. Want to see it?" When Tom asked for the woman's name, she said, "Just call me Alba Gal."

Tom Nelson had been salvaging orchids for several years, but until that day he had only heard vague rumors of an all-white *Cypripedium reginae*. He figured his chances of seeing such a flower were about as likely as hooking an albino muskie, but his skepticism evaporated the instant he laid eyes on the plant. Fearing that someone might steal the orchid, the woman had kept its location a secret until the day Tom walked into 9 Mile Bar. From roadhouse gossip up and down Highway 169, she already knew all about the orchid man's work. Her all-white wasn't for sale at any price but she was nervous about keeping it healthy. She wanted to know how to divide the plant and if it was possible to propagate cypripediums by seed. Tom promised not to reveal the location of the plant. That afternoon Alba Gal joined a growing number of local characters who alert Tom to endangered orchid sites, chase off illegal collectors, and help him dig plants when he is in the area. I should probably mention that apart from the illegality of collecting roadside orchids without proper permits, you definitely don't want to get caught poaching plants by local wildflower protectors such as Big Klink and Timmy White Eagle.

It wasn't until a year after this meeting at 9 Mile Bar that I first heard about Tom Nelson. My friend Richard Baskin, whom I had taken to Fire Mountain to look for *Paphiopedilum sanderianum* five years earlier, called to tell me that he had just met a man who was salvaging orchids from the roadside ditches of northern Minnesota. According to Richard, the man had proper permits and was legally selling the plants. Based on my six-year journey into the dark corners of the orchid world, this came as shocking news, and I couldn't imagine how he had managed the trick. I made a number of phone calls to the Minnesota Department of Agriculture and the Department of Transportation to check him out, and what I heard sounded too good to be true. In the second week of June 1999, I flew to Minneapolis to meet him. For the next six days, Tom Nelson, Richard, and I drove the back roads of northern Minnesota looking at threatened sites, digging plants, and learning firsthand how real orchid conservation works when the habitat can't be saved.

We drove north from Minneapolis past Mille Lacs, then on to Hay Point, Leech Lake, Deer River, and Lake Winnibigoshish. We rumbled by places like Thor's Sports Bar, the Hoot n' Holler Café, several Poochie Parlors, Arvin's Taxidermy, the Pine Cone Coffee House, the Frontier Steak and Cake Restaurant, the Cut and Wrap Shack, and tumbledown buildings with handwritten signs offering crawlers, shiners, suckers, fatheads, leeches, and live salamanders.

"Worst black fly hatch in sixty years," said a voice on the radio. We pulled into a convenience store for insect repellent.

There we also found an astonishing assortment of microwave pizzas, suntan lotions, Midnight Special rolling tobacco, Carmex lip balm, every fishing lure known to man or woman, camouflaged lawn chairs, personalized Styrofoam beer can holders, and enough bait and ammo to sustain an army of hunters and gatherers for several seasons.

As The Beast continued north, I thumbed through the pages of the county surveyors' map that Tom used as a navigational guide to the area. A quick perusal of the names of the property owners gave me a fair idea of what we were getting ourselves into. Within an hour, we would be entering the realm of Gaylan Paulish, Vern Hornbaker, Norval Tvelt, Elmer Hurlbutt, Bernie Plutko . . . and Gwyndale Fish.

One of the first unusual things I discovered about Tom was the fact that he is colorblind. Unlike Richard, who could identify the species and variety of flowering roadside plants while we drove by them at sixty miles an hour, Tom has to climb into the ditches and identify the flowers by their shape. I took an immediate liking to Tom Nelson because of his relaxed approach to collecting plants. He is never in a hurry. He feels that Mother Nature will provide, but I couldn't help noticing that Tom's plant rescue work is starting to take its toll on his back and knees. He still enjoys the work and the long lonely hours out on the road, but at age forty-seven he admits that orchid salvage in the north woods of Minnesota is better suited to a younger person.

Tom's preparation for an orchid rescue consists of throwing a tent and an unrolled sleeping bag into the back of his van along with shovels, plastic tubs, and nursery flats. He keeps a stack of his plant-collecting permits on the dashboard, but his day-to-day provisions amount to little more than a tin of Copenhagen snuff and at least two cases of Mountain Dew. There are so many gaping rust holes in the bottom of The Beast that Tom has gotten into the habit of watering down his salvaged plants with a hose without removing them from the back of the self-draining van. This year he started carrying a cellular phone, which he uses to contact local landowners and county agricultural inspectors to let them know exactly where he is, his permit numbers, and what time of day he will be collecting in their area.

The two-lane road that we were following meandered between towering walls of white pine. Before long The Beast broke cover and entered a stretch of stinking peat bogs still saturated by recent rain. The heat became oppressive, and by the time the windshield was well plastered with insects, Tom announced that we were getting into prime orchid country. On an unmarked country road, somewhere between the farm of Arvin Torgelson and Canada, Richard asked Tom how he got started in plant salvage.

"I used to teach middle school physics and chemistry, but on the weekends and during the summer months I did a bit of landscape gardening with nursery-grown native plants and local limestone. One day in 1994 I was up in this area and saw a construction crew rebuilding the shoulder of a road with a bulldozer. I know the different species and prices of woodland plants from my landscaping business, and in pretty short order I figured the crew destroyed about fifty thousand plants worth more than $300,000. That event had a big impact on my life."

After the road crew finished work for the day, Tom went back to the site for a closer look. He found the pulverized remains of plants, including the Minnesota state flower, *Cypripedium reginae*. Jumbled in with the debris were other protected woodland wildflowers such as columbine, wild ginger, star-flowered Solomon's seal, wild geranium, and several species of late-blooming trillium. Tom knew that it was illegal under state law to collect these plants and take them home, but he also realized that thousands more would die during the roadwork. Later that night, with a flashlight held in his mouth, Tom Nelson dug his first wild orchids and carefully replanted them at the tree line, where they would be safe.

"I just couldn't get it out of my mind," said Tom. "All those plants killed for no reason. When I got home, I started making phone calls to see if there was some way to legally rescue native plants from habitats that were going to be destroyed or developed." Tom carefully studied Minnesota Statute 17.28, the Wild Flower Act, but what really caught his attention was Statute 17.23, Conservation of Certain Wild Flowers. Statute 17.23, which dates back to 1925, provides guidelines and a permit-granting process that allows private citizens, under certain conditions, to collect wild plants. Tom applied for a permit, which was granted, but in the beginning the State Departments of Agriculture, Natural Resources, and Transportation kept a close eye on him. For the first year or so he was issued Department of Transportation permits that limited him to salvaging a total of eighteen "shovelfuls" per site. Many of the sites involved the destruction of tens of thousands of plants and round-trip road journeys of hundreds of miles, but Tom didn't complain. He persisted in salvaging his allotted eighteen "shovelfuls" per site. When he quit his teaching job his wife thought he had lost his mind.

The regulations allowed Tom to sell the salvaged plants to botanical institutions immediately, but he was required to grow the plants for a year before selling them to individuals or commercial nurseries. He obeyed the rules and kept most of them in his small backyard nursery. It eventually became clear to everyone involved that Tom's primary concern was native plant conservation, and that he had no interest in collecting plants from healthy habitats or pursuing short-term money-making schemes.

Road-working crews started calling Tom to let him know about upcoming projects. The 9 Mile Bar became an unlikely clearinghouse for rumors about threatened orchid habitats, and people at the Army Corps of Engineers also spotted potential sites. After a few years of scraping by, Tom was granted his first Minnesota Department of Agriculture Plant Protection Permit to collect unlimited numbers of all plant species in areas that would be destroyed.

Over the past few collecting seasons, Tom Nelson has legally salvaged more than 15,000 native orchids from dozens of sites around the state. More than half of this plant material is kept in a nursery where he selects the best plants for breeding, seed collection, cultivation, and propagation by division. He receives no public funds or grant money from conservation groups and is not affiliated with any orchid societies. He is blissfully ignorant of the petty politics that rule the orchid world. His entire operation is funded by the sale of plants to nature centers, arboretums, universities, and native-plant interest groups. A limited number of plants are also sold to a handful of carefully selected orchid nurseries in the United States and in Europe. In the United Kingdom, where the wild population of *Cypripedium calceolus* has been reduced to a single plant, there is a huge demand for Tom's salvaged North American cypripediums, which are now available to botanists, growers, and hobbyists through nurseries in Scotland and England.

I have to admit I was rather disappointed to hear all of this, because the primary purpose of my trip to Minnesota was to get the story on how a small-town visionary had successfully battled an army of entrenched bureaucrats who were bent on perpetuating misguided conservation laws that were contributing to the mass destruction of orchids growing in the wild. As it turned out, the Minnesota state Departments of Agriculture, Transportation, and Natural Resources had all been extremely helpful and accommodating. "They are great people to work with," Tom told me. "And U.S. CITES and the U.S. Department of Agriculture?" I asked. "Incredibly supportive and patient," Tom replied. I was dumbfounded to hear that government officials and a private citizen could actually work together and generate results. Once the truth sank in, I told Tom that after six years of searching, this was the first time I had come across a worthwhile, ongoing, legal, and self-sustaining orchid conservation project anywhere in the world. "Minnesotans are a practical people," he explained.

Within half an hour we arrived at our first collection site, a four-mile-long stretch of country road near Lake of the Woods. Tom usually works by himself, but with Richard and me along to help, we quickly developed an efficient way of locating the scattered plants, which were well hidden in the grass-filled drainage ditches. Our technique involved the use of the dozens of empty Mountain Dew cans that littered the floor of the van. Richard would stand in the open door of The Beast while Tom drove at about ten miles an hour. When Richard called out "Showies" or "Yellows," I threw one of the crushed Mountain Dew cans onto the roadside as a marker. We used Mountain Dew cans because they were easy to distinguish from the hundreds of thousands of empty beer cans that litter the roadsides of northern Minnesota. State law forbids open beer cans in vehicles. The law hasn't stopped drunk driving in Minnesota, but it has guaranteed that all empties are immediately thrown out the windows. At the end of the permitted section of road Tom would turn the van around so that we could mark the other side of the road. Once we knew where the plants were located, the van was parked and we set off on foot, shovels in hand. We followed the trail of Mountain Dew markers, dug up orchids, and collected our cans along the way.

For aspiring orchid collectors, or those of you who might think the collection process is easy, I should point out that before a single plant can be lifted from the ground, approximately two or three years can be spent identifying a potential site, counting the plants, securing the property owner's permission, and obtaining permits from the Minnesota Departments of Agriculture and Transportation. Once this has been done, Tom carefully prepares beds in his nursery to receive the salvaged plants, where they will grow for one to two years before they are inspected for pests and disease by the Department of Agriculture. After that, Tom can sell the plants.

Each year he only has a ten-to-twelve-week window of opportunity to locate and dig orchids. When a road has been designated for widening, anyone can apply for a collecting permit, but Tom is fourth in line behind educational institutions, landowners, and local garden clubs. Once he has the permit there is no guarantee that the salvage will be successful, because in a matter of hours illegal collectors can clear out a site that Tom has been studying for years. Even when everything goes as planned, a road construction crew facing a deadline might have to start work ahead of schedule; then all the plants might be lost because Tom can't get to the site in time to save them. On one project, he was forced to dig up orchids ten feet in front of an advancing line of falling trees as the bulldozers bore down on him. That evening, he concluded his paltry salvage by prying plants from between the tractor treads of giant earth-moving equipment.

"Some native-plant society people see red when they hear about me collecting and selling wild orchids. I imagine some of them would like to crush me like a bug, but I invite them to come walk the ditches, inspect the sites and my nursery, and only then do they get the picture that this is not a rape-the-earth program I'm running. Instead, it is a final respect to the plant community that is about to be destroyed."

Collecting wild orchids by the roadside might sound like a pleasant way to spend a Sunday afternoon, but in practice, an orchid salvage operation goes something like this. Once the permits have been issued, you drive several hundred miles on two-lane roads while keeping a sharp lookout for turnoffs that are not signposted and do not appear on any map. When you have located the permitted section of road, you park your vehicle at the nearest turnout or crossroad, which in most cases is several miles away because the unimproved country roads have no shoulders. The outer edge of the roadway simply drops off at a thirty-degree angle into a ten-foot-deep ditch. The orchids grow at the bottom of these ditches, which are often strewn with broken bottles, discarded tires, old refrigerators, rotting deer carcasses and other roadkill, household garbage, aluminum cans, and a stinking bog that can suck off your boots if you don't double-tie the laces. Even the most pristine, weed-covered ditches are alive with black flies, mosquitoes, ticks, horseflies, and deerflies, not to mention the thickets of poison ivy. If the ditch doesn't contain a large number of these horrors there probably aren't any orchids growing there. The plants, if you can find them, must be dug out of the muck with their heavy root balls intact and then lugged back to the vehicle as logging trucks, roaring by at seventy miles an hour on blind curves, pass within a few feet of you with their air horns blaring. Temperatures in the nineties with high humidity are not uncommon. As Tom Nelson likes to say, "These plants will teach you patience."

During our orchid survey of the north woods we usually spent the night in motels that had been built before World War II. The sad-looking rooms with their kitchenette and bathroom plumbing held together with duct tape had barely survived the years of seasonal visits by snowmobilers, hunters, and fishermen. Most of the furniture was bolted to the floor, and in some places the walls and hollow-core doors were battered from decades of flying fists and the headbutts of visiting sportsmen and their room guests. After a shower and dinner we would wander down to the local bar to mingle with the locals and play pool. Most of the people we met provided great entertainment and excellent conversation, but one night a short, drunk, belligerent man with stubby fingers and no neck staggered around the pool table and threatened us with violence because he thought we were making fun of him when we told him we had come to the area to collect wildflowers.

"I just don't get it, I just don't get it," the man muttered over and over again. In his mind, real men didn't collect wildflowers for a living. He convinced himself that we were undercover agents working for the U.S. Fish and Wildlife Service. He warned us that we were in rough country, but I had no idea how rough until later that night when I lay back on my bed at the Evergreen Motel and turned on the television. The screen flickered to life just as an autopsy was getting under way. A man in protective rubber clothing and a full-face spray shield cut off the top of a dead man's head with a power saw; while this was being done, I couldn't help but wonder what the man at the bar might do if he got his hands on a Fish and Wildlife agent posing as a wildflower collector.

Each day we moved from one site to the next, racking up the miles and collecting a couple of dozen orchids at one place, then maybe a half-dozen at the next. It was nearly impossible to spot the plants and the digging was just simple down-and-dirty hard physical grunt work. You can loosen the soil with a shovel, but then you have to get down on your hands and knees, sink your fingers into the black muck, and wrestle the plant from the sucking earth while trying not to inhale too many horseflies or mosquitoes.

Working in the ditches with Tom reminded me of my original idea to help the Penan people of Borneo build a small nursery and stock it with salvaged orchids and other rare plants from doomed habitats. The threats to the orchids in northern Minnesota and Borneo are practically identical, but by the time I met Tom Nelson I realized it was next to impossible for the indigenous people of Borneo to rescue plants from the forest. In the Borneo rain forest, logging operations, dam projects, huge land-clearing schemes for agriculture, road-building operations, and the quarrying of limestone for cement factories provide ample opportunities to salvage orchids and other rare plants from destruction. Unfortunately, local politics, lack of a domestic market for the plants, coupled with CITES-influenced trade restrictions that prohibit the export of rare and endangered plants, virtually guarantee that those plants will remain in the path of any bulldozer that might come their way.

Tom Nelson is not the only person in Minnesota who is concerned about saving orchids from destruction. A road-widening project completed in 1998 on Highway 11 illustrates how conflicting views on conservation can contribute to the destruction of these plants. The most scenic section of Highway 11 runs just south of Lake of the Woods, between Greenbush and Baudette. This seventy-eight-mile stretch of road is known as the Orchid Highway because of the large numbers of orchids that flowered along the roadside during the summer. People in the state Department of Natural Resources estimate that as many as five million orchids came into bloom along the road each year; local residents claim that twenty years ago the figure was closer to ten million.

The Canadian Pacific Railway runs parallel to and just north of Highway 11, and Tom believes that the crushed limestone beneath the tracks and in the roadbed of Highway 11 have created what he calls an artificially enhanced orchid habitat. The man-made drainage ditches and the calcareous nature of the limestone have altered the acidity of the water and soil, which in combination with the seasonal burning of brush by the track has produced an ideal environment for both *Cypripedium reginae* and *C. calceolus*. The orchids did not exist in such heavy concentrations before the railroad and highway were built, but once the plants started to grow in great numbers, the two-lane road was designated as a scenic wildflower highway. More people came to see the flowers, and this naturally increased the wear on the road. Logging trucks also gave the highway heavy use. In time the roadway had to be widened and brought up to state-mandated safety standards. Ironically, the roadwork to improve the Orchid Highway required the wholesale destruction of the orchids.

"People don't understand that the roadside orchids of Highway 11 did not originally grow there in such numbers," explained Tom. "The road workers and railway people created the habitat. It was only later that the orchids naturally seeded themselves from the fields and surrounding area."

Wherever the orchids might have come from, when it was time to widen the highway and salvage the plants, Tom was surprised to learn that a local wildflower group led by resident Laverne Norquist wanted to exclude him from the orchid rescue project. By the end of April 1998, Tom had already acquired his permit to salvage eighteen "shovelfuls" of orchids from along Highway 11 and was asking for unlimited rights, but this must have rubbed the local wildflower people the wrong way because he was later informed that his collecting must be confined to the south side of the road. This is the side of the road away from the railroad tracks, and it was thought that few if any orchids grew there.

The primary disagreement was over what would happen to the orchids once they were removed from the site. Norquist and the wildflower people wanted to collect the orchids, place them in a field for a short time, and then replant them the following year when the roadwork was completed. Tom, on the other hand, wanted to collect, propagate, and sell some of the plants. His feeling was that the roadside habitat would take years to recover before successful reintroduction could take place. By that time the orchids would have started to seed themselves naturally, as they had originally done when the road was first built. No one knew which approach was best, but from Tom's viewpoint the most important thing was to get the orchids out of the ground, because those left behind would certainly be killed. The only thing that everyone agreed on was the fact that there were more orchids in the roadside ditches of Highway 11 than anyone could possibly collect before the roadwork began.

In mid-May 1998 the State Department of Transportation decided that, since there were tens of thousands and possibly hundreds of thousands of orchids to be salvaged, it was ridiculous to limit Tom to eighteen "shovelfuls." They sent him a new permit that allowed him to collect unlimited numbers from the south side of the highway. "Hey . . . whatever works," he told the permitting officer.

The orchid rescue operation took place on the seven-mile stretch of Highway 11 between the towns of Williams and Roosevelt. During the event Norquist and the wildflower people took up position on the north side of the road with an army of trucks, schoolchildren, friends and family members, Boy Scouts, senior citizens, volunteers from the Minnesota Conservation Corps, and youthful offenders working off their community service time. The Department of Transportation provided them with bright orange vests and the local media got involved. Norquist proudly announced that people had come to help rescue the state flower "from as far away as Fargo and Duluth."

Meanwhile, on the south side of the road, Tom Nelson was sitting in The Beast listening to the end of a tape by Rockin' Dopsie and the Cajun Twisters. As the thundering zydeco accordion beat died down, he placed a pinch of Copenhagen snuff beneath his upper lip, stepped down from the van, grabbed a shovel, and started to dig. On the north side of the road plants were being excavated by the thousands, while Tom methodically walked his barren side of the road, digging what he could find. By noontime, Norquist's orchid army had marched to the horizon, while Tom continued to dig up the plants one by one. Despite being colorblind, he has a good eye for plants, and that day he managed to fill nearly half his van. Accounts vary as to what happened after that, but when Norquist noticed the number of plants in Tom's van she somehow got it into her head that he was collecting on "her" side of the road. "As if they didn't have more orchids than they knew what to do with," Tom laughed.

The orchid rescue continued throughout the weekend. By late Sunday Tom had finished with his side of the road, having managed to salvage more than 1,000 orchids. He was getting ready for the long drive home when he noticed an elderly woman standing by herself on the north side of the road. She was one of the collectors, but the others had left her behind and she was disoriented and suffering from dehydration. Tom pulled over and gave her water. As they talked, he noticed that there were still thousands of orchids left on the north side.

As Tom drove home through the night, he naturally got to thinking about the fate of the orchids that were left in the ground on the north side of the road. The road crew was due to begin construction soon. A few days later he spoke on the phone with officials at the state Departments of Agriculture and Transportation and with Laverne Norquist. His inquiries revealed that the orchid army had dug up more than 50,000 plants, which was all they could handle. Unfortunately, the remaining plants had to stay where they were, and be destroyed, because by the time Tom was given permission to work the north side of the road, he had run out of money and was unable to return before the road crew started work.

"I salute their valiant efforts," Tom told Richard and me. "They did one hell of a job. Moved an impressive number of plants, good organization, and it was great how they got the local kids to help out. But I don't understand their attitude about saving roadside wildflowers. There must have been twenty to thirty thousand orchids left behind, but these people were content to see the plants destroyed rather than let me collect a single orchid from the north side of the road."

Both Richard and I laughed and told Tom that he had not been singled out for punishment. We assured him that he was certainly not the first person to come up against this sort of nonsense. We gave him numerous examples of how the exact same pattern of thinking has prevented any attempt at orchid salvage in tropical rain forests around the world where slash-and-burn agricultural clearing, hydroelectric projects, logging, strip mining, and large-scale plantation schemes threaten orchid habitats. I told him that records show that people who are in positions to legislate responsible conservation laws or regulations have convinced themselves, for whatever reasons, that it is better to let the orchids and other plants die than to have them salvaged and sold. In the case of the rarest orchids on earth, not even a seed pod can be harvested and legally transported across international borders for commercial propagation.

Richard and I couldn't resist pointing out that despite more than twenty-five years of lavish international meetings and conferences of the CITES countries, resolutions and revisions of resolutions (and revisions of revised resolutions), self-serving publications, vanity press releases, multi-million-dollar expenditures for training personnel to stop smuggling, armed raids on commercial orchid nurseries and hobbyists, and huge fines and jail sentences, as well as unsuccessful reintroduction schemes carried out with extravagance and vast expense, and high-tech GIS satellite surveys of potential orchid habitats, there was simply no reliable data to support the arguments that CITES and similar efforts had reduced smuggling, saved any orchid species from extinction, helped protect orchid habitats, or even salvaged orchid plants facing the certain destruction of their habitats. The contrast between this activity and Tom's work in northern Minnesota is profound. It is also worthy of careful study.

I told Tom and Richard about the time I asked the plants officer at the CITES headquarters in Geneva (the authority on the interpretation and implementation of the world's trade laws to protect orchids) how many plants had been saved as a result of regulating the international orchid trade over the past twenty-five years.

"And how many plants have they saved?" Tom wanted to know.

"He told me he didn't have a clue," I said.

The last orchid site that Tom showed us was a place called the Toivola Bog. This is a seventy-mile-wide black spruce and tamarack bog that is the source of some of the finest sphagnum moss on earth. The moss-mining company, Northwoods Organics, leases about 350 acres of the peat bog, which they prepare for harvesting by clearing and trenching. Once the groundwater has been drained, the surface of the moss field dries up. It is then scraped and fluffed up by huge tractors that move slowly over the fields. The very top surface of the field is picked up by gigantic vacuuming machines, then deposited in mounds that are taken away by truck for bagging and shipping. The peat moss is sold to garden centers, but most of it ends up on golf courses throughout the Midwest. Three hundred and fifty acres may sound like a large area, but when the operation is seen from the air it becomes clear that the company is merely nibbling at the edge of a vast area. When the groundwater in the old fields is allowed to return to its normal height, the sphagnum moss begins growing again and in time the habitat will regenerate itself. Once the manager of Northwoods Organics understood the nature of Tom's salvage work, he gave him free rein to study the habitat within the company's area of operation.

Tom brought us to Toivola Bog because this is where the orchid *Cypripedium acaule* grows by the untold millions. The nutrient-poor, spongy moss floor of the forest has a pH of about 3.5, which results in a stunted forest filled with orchids. Toivola Bog is also the home of some of the worst black flies and mosquitoes in northern Minnesota.

We parked the van and walked a short distance into the bog. It was a hot, muggy, overcast day, the forest had an eerie sameness to it, and without the sun to help gauge direction I immediately became disoriented. The damp forest floor was carpeted with a spongy layer of living moss; this meant that our footprints disappeared behind us. We kept in voice contact and wandered off in different directions, but a short while later I came upon Tom kneeling in the forest and muttering to himself. He looked as if he was in prayer, on his knees with his hands cupped in front of him, marveling at the fragile beauty of a *Cypripedium acaule* in full bloom.

I had never seen an acaule. The first thing I noticed was its sexy pink pouch covered with a fine downy fuzz. The pouch is divided into a pair of slightly wrinkled and parted lips. The flower is described as glandular pubescent, and at a glance I understood why. Richard joined us a few minutes later and Tom explained how the flower was pollinated by a bumblebee. The pink "one-way" lips part under the weight of the insect, and then close behind it. Once inside the pouch the bumblebee is forced to climb out of one of the twin openings near the top of the flower, where the insect collects or deposits pollen.

Tom estimated that more than 500,000 cypripediums are being destroyed in northern Minnesota and Wisconsin each year by road building, agricultural clearing, moss mining, or the construction of shopping malls, parking lots, golf courses, and residential developments. As Richard and I listened to him talk we could hear the nearby grumbling sounds of tractors and the huge vacuuming machines that were moving across the dry peat fields just beyond the tree line.

"What it boils down to is this," Tom said, once we had returned to the road. "Is it better to move the plants or leave them in the ground to be pulverized by a bulldozer? I'm not willing to stand by and watch it happen and I don't have a whole lot of time for people who can't work that one out. It's important to make the roads safe, and the moss miners have a legitimate right to harvest the peat. I can't do much about urban sprawl, but no way is anyone going to convince me that these orchids should be killed because they are too endangered to salvage.

"I save orchids for a living. That's what I do. I know there are people out there that would like to take me down and take me down hard, because they just can't tolerate the thought that there might be a simple solution to the problem. I own three shovels and The Beast, and as long as I can pull my permits and get landowners' permission I'm going to be walking ditches, digging plants, and wrestling root balls. The experts can debate their cutting-edge conservation theories all they like. I don't begrudge them, but I'll let you in on a little secret. You see over there where the peat field meets the forest? That's what I call the cutting edge. It's coming in this direction and the best way to save an orchid around here is with a permit, a shovel, and a bit of elbow grease."

Acknowledgments

This book could not have been written without the help of many people, especially Dick Sonnen, who first introduced me to the orchid world and then led me to many of the people and places that appear in these pages.

Kim Brown, who made the journey to Fire Mountain in Borneo possible. Joe Speiler and everyone at Pantheon, especially Dan Frank, Edward Kastenmeier, Altie Karper, Joy Dallanegra-Sanger, Sophie Cottrell, Suzanne Williams, Jeanne Morton, and Amelia Zalcman.

Those who critiqued the chapters in progress, and reviewed the final manuscript: Cindy Hill, Bruce MacBryde, Shelley Washburn, Roger Beck, Alice Erb, Carlo A. Balistrieri, and Bonnie Baskin. Thanks also to Bruce Stutz, Jenny Lawrence, Judy Rice, and Vittorio Maestro at *Natural History* magazine, where early versions of the chapters on orchid ice cream and *Coryanthes speciosa* first appeared.

The orchid people: Eleanor Kerrigan; Valerie Henderson at the Rod McLellen Company; Greer, Terre, Mark, and Terry at the Orchid Zone; the legendary Norris Powell at The Orchid House; Isabelle Bert and Marcel Lecoufle; Harry Zelenko in New York; orchid taxonomists Eric Christiansen and Guido Braem; Dr. Phyllis Nibbler in Zambia; the intrepid orchid hunter and jungle traveler Richard Baskin; Au Yong at Orchidwoods; Michael and Teresa Fung at Maisie Orchids; Xavier in Paris; Felix and Isabelle Saez in Caracas and Miami; Mike Morgan; Mary Nesbit; Joe

Kunisch of Bloomfield Orchids; Andy at Andy's Orchids; Harold Koopowitz and Norito Hasegawa at Paphanatics; Kerry Richards at A World of Orchids; Alan Koch at Gold Country Orchids; Kevin Porter; Paul Phillips at Ratcliffe Orchids; The Eric Young Foundation; the late Don Herman; Tom and Connie Nelson at Woods End Nursery; Ned Nash, president of the American Orchid Society; Ernest Hetherington; Rebecca Northen for her books on home orchid growing and for her comments on habitat destruction and orchid conservation; Sandro Cusi at Orquideas Río Verde in Mexico; the late Teódulo Chávez; Katja Anker and Hans Christiansen in Denmark; the late Jack Fowlie; John Beaman for his candid comments on how CITES adversely affects legitimate growers and scientists; the late Arturo Kolopaking; Fumi Sugiami; Henry Azadehdel, Harto Kolopaking, Koos Wubben, Bosha Popow, and the orchid hunters, collectors, and breeders that cannot be mentioned by name; Kemal Kucukonderuzunkoluk in Turkey; Katsuhiko Tokuda at Shiseido; and Minnesota wildflower protector Timmy White Eagle of the 9 Mile Bar.

The support crew in Sarawak and Sabah: Tony Lamb, Paul Chai at the Forestry Department in Kuching, Philip Yong, Ch'ien Lee, Isabelle Bijon, Tiong and the snake, Bati, Nyaru, Katong, Thomas Damit, Willie, Veno Envar, and Jenny Mallang.

Barbara Pitschel, head librarian at the San Francisco Botanical Gardens; Margaret Ramsey, Gren Lucas, Noel McGough, and Peter Wyse Jackson at Kew.

And finally, a special note of thanks to Ms. Sylvia FitzGerald, the head of Library and Archives at the Royal Botanic Gardens, Kew, who greatly aroused my curiosity in the case of Henry Azadehdel when she informed me that I would have to wait thirty years before I could examine the file containing his personal correspondence with Kew botanists.

Bibliography

Ackerman, J.D. "Phenological Relationships of Male Euglossine Bees and Their Orchid Fragrance Hosts." Ph.D. thesis, Wisconsin University, 1981.

———. "Specificity and Mutual Dependency of the Orchid–Euglossine Bee Interaction." *Biological Journal of the Linnean Society* 20 (1983): 301–14.

Arctander, S. *Perfume and Flavor Materials of Natural Origin.* Elizabeth, N.J.: S. Arctander, 1960.

Arditti, Joseph, ed. *Orchid Biology: Reviews and Perspectives.* 7 vols. Vols. 1–4, Ithaca, N.Y.: Cornell University Press, 1977–87. Vol. 5, Portland, Ore.: Timber Press, 1991. Vol. 6, New York: John Wiley, 1994. Vol. 7, Norwell, Mass.: Kluwer Academic, 1997.

Baker, Charles O., and Baker, Margaret. *Orchid Species Culture: Pescatorea to Pleione.* Portland, Ore.: Timber Press, 1991.

———. *Orchid Species Culture: Dendrobium.* Portland, Ore.: Timber Press, 1996.

Beaman, J., and Woods, J. J. *The Plants of Mount Kinabalu,* Vol. 2, *Orchids.* Kew: Royal Botanic Gardens, 1993.

Bechtel, Helmut; Cribb, Phillip; and Launert, Edmund. *The Manual of Cultivated Orchid Species.* 3rd ed. Cambridge, Mass.: MIT Press, 1992.

Braem, Guido; Baker, Charles O.; and Baker, Margaret. *The Genus Paphiopedilum: Natural History and Cultivation.* Kissimmee, Fla.: Botanical Publishers, vol. 1, 1998; vol. 2, 1999.

————. *Paphiopedilum: A Monograph of All Tropical and Subtropical Asiatic Slipper Orchids.* Hildesheim: Sprücke Verlag, 1988.

Chan, C. L.; Lamb, A.; Shim, P.S.; and Wood, J. J. *Orchids of Borneo. Vol. 1, Introduction and a Selection of Species.* Kew: Royal Botanic Gardens, 1994.

Cribb, Phillip. *The Genus Paphiopedilum.* 2nd ed. Kew: Royal Botanic Gardens, 1999.

Darwin, Charles. *The Various Contrivances by Which Orchids Are Fertilized by Insects.* London: John Murray, 1862.

Desmond, Ray. *Kew: The History of the Royal Botanic Gardens.* London: Harvill, 1995.

————. *Sir Joseph Dalton Hooker: Traveller and Plant Collector.* London: Antique Collectors' Club, 1999.

Dobson, H. C. M. "Role of Flower and Pollen Aromas in Host-Plant Recognition by Solitary Bees." *Oecologia* 72 (1987): 618–23.

Dressler, Robert L. *The Orchids: Natural History and Classification.* Cambridge, Mass.: Harvard University Press, 1981.

Dunsterville, G. C. K., and Dunsterville, E. *Orchid Hunting in the Lost World (and elsewhere in Venezuela).* West Palm Beach, Fla.: American Orchid Society, 1988.

Dunsterville, G. C. K., and Garay, L. A. *Venezuelan Orchids Illustrated.* 6 vols. London: André Deutsch, 1958–76.

Hágsater, Eric, and Dumont, Vinciane. *Orchids: Status Survey and Conservation Action Plan.* Gland, Switzerland, and Cambridge, U.K.: IUCN/SSC Orchid Specialist Group, 1996.

Hunt, P. Francis. *The Orchid.* New York: Mayflower Books, 1978.

Kaiser, Roman. *The Scent of Orchids: Olfactory and Chemical Investigations.* Amsterdam: Elsevier, 1993.

Keenan, Phillip E. *Wild Orchids Across North America: A Botanical Travelogue.* Portland, Ore.: Timber Press, 1998.

Koopowitz, Harold, and Kaye, Hilary. *Plant Extinction: A Global Crisis.* Washington, D.C.: Stone Wall Press, 1983.

Lawler, L. J. "Ethnobotany of the Orchidaceae," in Joseph Arditti, ed., *Orchid Biology: Reviews and Perspectives, vol. 3,* pp. 27–149. Ithaca, N.Y.: Cornell University Press, 1984.

Nagano, Y. "History of Orchid Growing in Japan." *American Orchid Society Bulletin* 22, no. 5 (1953).

Northen, Rebecca. *Home Orchid Growing.* 4th rev. ed. New York: Prentice-Hall, 1990.

Pridgeon, Alec, ed. *The Illustrated Encyclopedia of Orchids.* Portland, Ore.: Timber Press, 1992.

Reinikka, Merle A., and Romero, G. *A History of the Orchid.* Rev. ed. Portland, Ore.: Timber Press, 1995.

Roubik, David W. *Ecology and Natural History of Tropical Bees.* New York: Cambridge University Press, 1989.

Seidenfaden, G., and Wood, J. J. *The Orchids of Peninsular Malaysia and Singapore.* Fredensborg: Olsen and Olsen, 1992.

Shuttleworth, F. S.; Dillion, G. W.; and Zim, H. S. *Golden Guide to Orchids*. Rev. ed. New York: Western Publishing, 1989.

Stewart, J. "Orchid Conservation: The Survival and Maintenance of Genetic Diversity of All Orchids Throughout the World," in K. Saito and R. Tanaka, eds., *Proceedings from the 12th World Orchid Conference*, 1987, pp. 106–9.

Wijnstekers, W. *The Evolution of CITES*. Rev. ed. Geneva: CITES Secretariat, 1992.

Williams, N. H., and Dodson, C. H. "Selective Attraction of Male Euglossine Bees to Orchid Floral Fragrances and Its Importance in Long-Distance Pollen Flow." *Evolution* 26 (1983): 84–95.

About the Author

Eric Hansen is the author of *Stranger in the Forest* and *Motoring with Mohammed.* He lives in San Francisco.